1975

GE
Duk
The
3 0301 00016013 1

THE PUBLIC SCHOOLS AND RELIGION

may be kept

DAYS

SISTER M. AMBROSE, O.S.F.

EXPLORATION SERIES IN EDUCATION

*Under the Advisory Editorship of John Guy Fowlkes
and Edward A. Krug*

THE PUBLIC SCHOOLS
AND RELIGION:
THE LEGAL CONTEXT

SAM DUKER

Brooklyn College of the City University of New York

HARPER & ROW, Publishers, New York

LIBRARY
College of St. Francis
JOLIET, ILL.

THE PUBLIC SCHOOLS AND RELIGION: The Legal Context
Copyright © 1966 by Sam Duker
Printed in the United States of America. All rights reserved.
No part of this book may be used or reproduced in any
manner whatsoever without written permission except in the
case of brief quotations embodied in critical articles and re-
views. For information address Harper & Row, Publishers,
Incorporated, 49 East 33rd Street, New York, N.Y. 10016.

LIBRARY OF CONGRESS CATALOG CARD NUMBER: 66–10112

340
D876

CONTENTS

71633

CASES EXCERPTED AND DISCUSSED

EDITORS' INTRODUCTION

L<small>IKE ALL MATTERS</small> of importance, the relationship between religion and education, particularly public education, deeply affects people with respect to their most cherished values and beliefs. Objective study of such matters is not easily come by, and earnest advocates on all sides of the church-state question have been noted less for their inquiry than for their eloquence. There has been much tendency to seek resolution of the issue through formulas and slogans. No group or party has had a monopoly on this practice.

Some aspects of the question, however, do lend themselves to relatively dispassionate inquiry. One of these is the identification of what the Supreme Court of the United States has declared to be the meaning of those parts of the Constitution that pertain to the relationship at hand. Another is accurate rendition of the ways in which the Court has applied this meaning to a variety of specific issues, including public financial aid to religious schools, the impact of such exercises as the salute to the flag on the religious convictions of public-school pupils, released time for religious instruction, and the conduct of religious exercises in the public schools themselves.

In this book Professor Duker has supplied the essential materials for study of both these aspects. One may or may not agree with what the Court has said, but what it has said should be understood. The judgments of the Court have established on many specific questions what may and may not be done according to the Constitution as it now stands. Meanwhile, of course, our citizens are free to advocate and work for whatever changes in the Constitution they see as desirable, or, equally, to oppose and work against such changes.

Professor Duker has chosen an unusual and effective approach to this presentation. He has provided careful and objective commentary on major decisions along with substantial portions of the texts. This book should be of great value to students in a variety of courses in history, education, and political theory, and to the general reader as well.

JOHN GUY FOWLKES
EDWARD A. KRUG

May 18, 1965

· PREFACE

R<small>ECENT</small> <small>DECISIONS</small> of the Supreme Court of the United States dealing with the relationship of religion and the schools have been the subject of extensive comments, both favorable and unfavorable. It is an unfortunate fact that most of the readers of these comments and in many cases the commentators themselves have not read the actual decisions but base their judgments on what they have heard or read from other sources.

This state of affairs is possibly attributable to the fact that while the opinions of the Supreme Court are readily available, they are often very lengthy and frequently deal extensively with legal technicalities that are not of general interest.

It is the purpose of this book to present a meaningful selection of the language used by the Justices of the Supreme Court in deciding issues relating to religion and the schools.

Twelve cases coming before the Supreme Court have been selected for this purpose. In all but three instances the cases are decided on the basis of an interpretation of the Establishment and Free Exercise clauses of the First Amendment to the

United States Constitution. The three other cases (*Meyer*, *Pierce*, and *Cochran*) are included because the fundamental decisions there rendered form a basis for subsequent First Amendment cases.

The first two cases from which excerpts are given are *Meyer v. Nebraska*, dealing with the right of a state to prohibit the teaching of foreign languages in nonpublic schools, and *Pierce v. Society of Sisters*, which dealt with the validity of an Oregon statute requiring all children to attend public school classes.

Next, two cases having to do with an interpretation of the Free Exercise Clause of the First Amendment are included. (All the remaining cases dealt with the Establishment Clause.) Here the Supreme Court first held in *Gobitis* that states had the right to require public school pupils to participate in the flag salute—but then reversed itself in *Barnette*.

The child benefit theory was established in *Cochran* and *Everson*, which are next excerpted in Chapter 5. In Chapter 6 the *McCollum* and *Zorach* cases, having to do with released time for religious instruction during school hours, are discussed.

Chapter 7 has to do with the well-known 1962 decision in *Engel v. Vitale* which held that the recitation of a state-composed prayer in public school classrooms is a violation of the Establishment Clause. Finally, Chapter 8 considers the *Schempp*, *Murray* and *Chamberlin* cases in which the Engel doctrine was expanded.

An effort has been made to include only a minimum of technical legal discussion. Cases cited by the Justices in their opinions have largely been omitted. Some cases are referred to without giving their citations but proper references to all cases included may be found in the Table of Cases at the end of this book.

Those interested in pursuing the subject matter further will find a vast literature available. Only a few of the many items included have been selected for the very brief bibliography, but it is hoped that these will serve as an adequate beginning to an extended study.

It is not the purpose of this book to participate in the controversy as to the "rightness" or "wrongness" of the decisions of the Supreme Court in these cases. Opinions differ sharply on this point but holders of all viewpoints can, I think, profit from an examination of the reasoning employed by the Court in reaching its decisions.

SAM DUKER

THE PUBLIC SCHOOLS AND RELIGION

CHAPTER 1

INTRODUCTION

. . . we think that the constitutional prohibition against laws respecting an establishment of religion must at least mean that in this country it is no part of the business of government to compose official prayers for any group of American people to recite as part of a religious program carried on by government.

THIS STATEMENT is found in the majority opinion of the Supreme Court of the United States in the now famous case of *Engel* v. *Vitale*, decided in June 1962. The decision in that case outlawing the use of a prayer sponsored by the New York State Board of Regents in the public schools aroused much controversy. Many people were sincerely disturbed, while others heartily approved of the outcome of the case. Needless to say, the lunatic fringe also found this an opportunity to have its say.

Only a year later, in June 1963, the Supreme Court cleared up many of the questions that had arisen in the minds of students of the *Vitale* case and decided that a state cannot constitutionally hold religious exercises in public school classrooms even when the majority of the persons affected favor the exercises. At issue was the reading of passages from the Bible and the recitation of the Lord's Prayer.

The appropriate relationship between religious activities and the schools has two aspects. The first legal aspect is one that must be resolved, ultimately, by the courts of the several states and in appropriate cases by the federal courts. The second aspect is one of policy, which must be resolved by local and state authorities. Policy, however, cannot conflict with legal rulings.

In this discussion we are concerned primarily with only one limited view of the legal aspect. We shall deal here only with those cases having to do with this issue that were decided by the Supreme Court of the United States. We shall not, except in passing, be concerned with matters of local or state policy, or with matters involving only state laws, or with the provisions of state constitutions.

In this book there are excerpts from and discussions of 12 decisions of the Supreme Court of the United States dealing with the relationship between religion and the schools insofar as the provisions of the federal Constitution are involved.

It is not the purpose of this book to reach any conclusions about the merits or demerits of these decisions. Comments will be made only to clarify for the lay reader what was involved in each case and what was actually decided by the Court.

Certain basic legal principles are involved in gaining an understanding of the Supreme Court decisions that will be dealt with in this book. It is the purpose of this chapter to give brief explanations of these principles.

EDUCATION AS A STATE RATHER THAN A FEDERAL CONCERN

The Tenth Amendment of the Constitution of the United States was adopted in 1791 along with the first nine amendments as a part of what is commonly referred to as the Bill of Rights. It reads as follows:

Powers not delegated, reserved to states and people respectively. The powers not delegated to the United States by the Constitution, nor prohibited by it to the States, are reserved by the States respectively, or to the people.

This amendment clearly makes education a state matter as there is no provision dealing with it in the Constitution. It follows, therefore, that the overwhelming number of legal cases dealing with educational or school matters will be finally decided in the state courts. The federal courts become involved in law cases having to do with education in the several states only when there is a claim that the case involves a provision of the Constitution of the United States. All of the cases involved in this book concern the validity of acts of school or state authorities in the light of the provisions of the federal Constitution.

THE FIRST AMENDMENT

Most important for our purpose are the provisions of the First Amendment which state in part:

Congress shall make no law respecting an establishment of religion or prohibiting the free exercise thereof.

Two points should be noted in reading this provision. First, this is a prohibition on the federal government and not on the states; and second, there are two separate prohibitions: (1) against the establishment of religion; and (2) against the interference with the free exercise of religion.

In 1833 the Supreme Court, speaking through Chief Justice John Marshall in *Barron* v. *Baltimore*, unequivocally refused to interpret the Bill of Rights in such a way as to affect state action. The federal Constitution, the opinion stated, was "ordained and established by the people of the United States for themselves, for their own government, and not for the gov-

ernment of the individual states." This doctrine was reaffirmed
in a number of later cases.

In 1868 the Fourteenth Amendment was adopted. In
part, this amendment stated: "No State shall make or enforce
any law which shall abridge the privileges and immunities of
citizens of the United States; . . ."

As a result of the passage of this amendment it was natural that the question should arise as to what "the privileges and
immunities of citizens of the United States" consisted of. Beginning in 1875, in a number of cases, the Supreme Court repeatedly held that they did not include the guaranties in the
federal Bill of Rights. As early as 1892, however, dissenting opinions began to urge the contrary view—that is, that the Fourteenth Amendment was intended to make all of the federal
Bill of Rights applicable to the states. This view has been consistently advanced by Justice Black since 1947 but has never
been adopted by a majority of the Court.

The Fourteenth Amendment also states in a passage
immediately following the one just quoted: ". . . nor shall any
State deprive any person of life, liberty, or property, without due
process of law; . . ." Under this provision certain parts of the
federal Bill of Rights have been held to be applicable to the
states. In the case of *Cantwell v. Connecticut* (1940) the First
Amendment's protections for religion were held to be applicable to the states as well as to the federal government.

Most of the cases dealt with in this book are concerned
with the Establishment Clause and the Freedom of Exercise
provision of the First Amendment. It should be noted that the
phrase, "separation of church and state" does not appear in the
Constitution.

HOW CASES REACH THE
SUPREME COURT

Most cases involving questions concerning religious activities in relation to the school are settled in the trial court, as

are most other cases. A trial court is a court of "original juris-diction" which takes testimony and reaches a decision on the basis of the facts found and the law as interpreted by it. Un-less an appeal is taken, the decision of the trial court is final insofar as that particular case is concerned. In order to prevent a proliferation of litigation there is a legal principle, *res adjudi-cata* (the matter has been decided), which prevents the same case from being brought to the courts again. There are several reasons why appeals are usually not taken, the principal one being the heavy expense involved in attorneys' fees and court costs.

When an appeal is taken from a decision of the state trial court it goes to one of several courts, depending upon the laws of the particular state where the case has been brought. The decisions of the judges of these appellate courts and the reasons for their decisions are printed and are available in law libraries. The decisions of the trial courts are, with unimportant exceptions, not generally available. In only a very few instances, and then only when a federal constitutional question is involved, is a case taken beyond the state's highest appellate court. In these instances a request to hear the case is made to the Supreme Court of the United States. Because of the heavy demands of this Court only a small percentage of these requests is granted. The Justices of the Supreme Court spend much time in decid-ing which cases present issues important enough to warrant the Court's acceptance of the case. No one has an absolute right to have his case heard by the Supreme Court.

When a constitutional question is involved it is also possible for the suit to be brought to the federal trial court, which is the United States District Court. There are 88 of these district courts located throughout the United States.

Cases in the United States District Courts are ordinarily heard and decided (with or without a jury depending on the type of case presented) by one district judge. When the constitu-tionality of state action is involved, however, a three-judge court must be convened.

Appeals from the district courts ordinarily go to one of the ten Circuit Courts of Appeals. These courts, under usual circumstances, are the final appellate courts in federal cases, but when two or more of these Circuit Courts of Appeals differ on the law applicable to identical or closely similar cases, the Supreme Court will often accept jurisdiction to resolve this difference. Exceptional cases are accepted even in the absence of such a conflict when the Supreme Court deems the issues involved to be of sufficient general importance. Under certain circumstances the Supreme Court will accept a case on the basis of a district court's decision without the intervening appeal to the circuit court.

It can be seen from the preceding paragraphs that the road to a Supreme Court hearing is a long and devious one and that the likelihood of any given case obtaining such a hearing is a very slim one indeed.

There is a mistaken impression that the Supreme Court's refusal to accept a case necessarily denotes approval of the ruling of the lower court. This is true in some cases but it is not always so as the Court may refuse to take jurisdiction for a number of other reasons which may or may not be specifically stated by the Court. This principle is aptly illustrated by the case of *Doremus* v. *Board of Education* (1952), which we will discuss briefly after a short explanation of the principle of "mootness."

MOOT CASES

With very few exceptions, courts will not decide hypothetical cases. When there is no genuine issue subject to decision a case is called "moot" and the courts will refuse to go further with it. The reasons for this rule or policy are readily apparent. The advocacy of a genuine case is much more likely to be thorough and painstaking than the advocacy of a hypothetical or imaginary case. If principles were laid down in a moot case it would to some extent determine the rights of future litigants having real issues at stake concerning the same or similar situations. The parties would thus, in effect, be deprived of the opportunity to present their cases.

Another and equally cogent reason for the rule about mootness is that already overburdened courts would be subjected to an intolerable amount of additional work if they were obliged to decide hypothetical cases as well as those having real issues.

THE *DOREMUS* CASE

This was a New Jersey case that involved the issue of whether daily reading of passages from the Bible in public school classrooms under a state statute requiring such reading was consonant with the provisions of the First Amendment. The highest court in New Jersey decided that there was no conflict and the case was then carried to the Supreme Court of the United States. This court refused to consider the case on the grounds that the youngster whose parents had brought the suit had, during the course of the litigation, been graduated from the school and that there was, therefore, no longer a real issue and that the case had thus become moot. It was then argued that the parents should be allowed to carry on the litigation as taxpayers but this claim was also rejected by the Court. This rejection was based on the plaintiff's lack of "standing to sue." In order to prevent an inordinate excess of litigation the rule is that one not having a direct interest or one who is not likely to suffer injury does not have "standing" to complain.

The *Doremus* case is a good illustration of an important principle that must be kept in mind continually while reading the cases in this book. It is just as important in understanding and interpreting these decisions to be aware of what the Court did *not* say or did *not* pass on as it is to note what the Court *did* say and *did* pass on. The *Doremus* case has often been cited, erroneously, as indicating approval by the Supreme Court of the reading of the Bible in public school classrooms. However, since the refusal to hear this case rested on entirely different grounds, there was no indication whatsoever in this decision of the view of the Supreme Court on the question of Bible reading in the public school.

The *Doremus* case illustrates one other principle. This is that the Supreme Court will not reach and decide a constitutional question unless an answer to that question is essential to the disposition of the case at issue. In fact, decisions are, theoretically, as narrow as possible and deal only with the particular facts involved in the particular case at bar.

OBITER DICTUM

Now it is true that Justices, being human, sometimes find themselves unable to refrain from making more generalized statements in their written opinions than are strictly called for by the case at issue. Such statements are called obiter dicta (remarks in passing) and do not have the same binding effect on the Court in deciding future cases that the decision on the actual case has. Sometimes, however, a case may be best remembered and most often cited because of the contents of its dicta.

STARE DECISIS

In order to maintain some stability, a legal doctrine of *stare decisis* (let the decision stand) is part of the framework of our legal system. This simply means that courts will, as a rule, follow their previous decisions. Thus, the Supreme Court will ordinarily follow the "precedent" set by its previous decisions and lower courts are bound to follow such decisions. It can readily be seen that if it were not for the stabilizing influence of this rule chaos would result. It would be impossible for attorneys to advise their clients as to their rights and often the decision of whether or not to pursue an appeal would assume the nature of a game of chance. The legal requirement that "ignorance of the law is no excuse" would also become meaningless.

Technically, a case is only a precedent insofar as the particular facts and issues of that case are concerned. Actually, because of this principle, a decided case and the reasons given for the decision bear great weight in analogous cases as well.

WHEN *STARE DECISIS* IS NOT APPLICABLE

There is, however, a degree of flexibility in the application of the doctrine of *stare decisis*. We are speaking here specifically of the Supreme Court of the United States but the application of these exceptions is general in all courts. There are several ways in which a previous decision may be changed:

1. The Court may decide to overrule and thus change a previous decision. An example of this is given in Chapter 5 in the flag salute cases. Here, the Court in 1940, decided that requiring children in public school classes to take part in the Pledge of Allegiance was not in violation of the free exercise of religion clause of the First Amendment even when it was claimed that this ceremony was contrary to the religious beliefs of certain children and their parents. Then, only three years later in 1943, the Supreme Court decided that the first decision had been in error and in so many words overruled the previous decision. Such direct overruling of previous decisions seldom occurs.

2. More frequently the Court will distinguish a closely related set of facts in a current case from those in a previously decided case. An example of this may be found in Chapter 4 dealing with the two cases on released time for religious instruction. Here the two cases were quite similar but opposite conclusions were reached as to the law applicable on the basis of a distinction in the facts involved in the two cases. Justice Black in his dissenting opinion in the second case stated: "I

see no significant difference between the invalid Illinois system
and that of New York here sustained." Obviously, the majority
of the Court felt justified in their view that there was a real
difference in the facts presented by the two cases.

3. Least frequent of all is a change of decision as the
result of an immediate rehearing granted the losing party. None
of the decisions discussed in this book were reached in this
manner.

THE LAW'S DELAYS

There is a saying that "Justice delayed is justice denied."
Unfortunately, the process of litigation is often long and drawn
out. Calendars of trial courts are, as a general rule, quite heavy
and there is an almost inevitably long delay from the time a suit
is first instituted until the case is tried. The trial in a case involving delicate issues as are inherent in cases of the type dealt with
here are often prolonged and the judge may take some time to
arrive at his difficult decision.

After the trial court has terminated a case the process of
appeal is again lengthy. Transcripts of the trial proceedings must
be prepared, briefs written, and often oral arguments made before the case is submitted to the appellate court for decision.
The dockets of these appellate courts are invariably crowded and
as a result delays occur not only before a case is heard, but also
after it is heard to enable judges to agree on a decision and to
write their opinions.

When a case is finally carried to the Supreme Court of
the United States it has already gone through the process of
trial and usually one or more previous appeals. The work of the
Supreme Court is also very heavy and another long delay occurs
here in placing the case on the calendar, hearing oral arguments,
considering written briefs filed by the opposing parties, and in
preparing the opinions after the Court's ruling is decided. In
some cases a party not privy to the case may, on the ground of

his interest in the outcome, be permitted to appear as *amicus curiae* (friend of the court) in order to present his views to the Court in oral or written form.

The result is a long lapse of time between the decision to institute legal action and the final adjudication by the Supreme Court. As we have seen in our discussion of the *Doremus* case, some matters even become moot during the inevitably long period of litigation.

It is easier to regret these delays than it is to find a solution to this problem. Recently, the federal court system has been considerably expanded in terms of number of judges. It is hoped that this expansion may in some degree diminish the extent of delays but unfortunately, as our country grows, the load of litigation also grows and it is a race to see whether the expansion of the courts will be able to keep ahead of the growth in the number of law cases.

In the next chapter some of the unresolved questions concerning religious activities and schools are discussed. It should be apparent from the preceding paragraphs that there is no great likelihood that all or even most of these issues will be resolved by the Supreme Court within the immediate future.

WHEN JUSTICES DISAGREE

In almost all of the cases included in this book the decisions were not unanimous. Often, the division of the Court is very close, being 5 to 4 in a number of cases. The first thoughtless tendency is to feel that this amounts to a decision by one Justice rather than by the Court as a whole. While it cannot be denied that a change of judgment by one Justice would have altered the final decision, it must be remembered that the decision was really reached by the concurrence of five Justices rather than by one.

Obviously, the expense and time involved in carrying a case to the Supreme Court is not lightly undertaken. Equally apparent is the extreme likelihood that learned counsel on both sides of the case had advised their clients that there was a reasonable chance of success. If counsel can and do differ it is not surprising that Justices are also, on occasion, unable to agree. The law is not a jigsaw puzzle with a foreordained solution; it is rather a complex admixture of precedent, justice, philosophy, and interpretation.

When the Justices of the Supreme Court have agreed on a majority decision, one of the Justices who is part of that majority is assigned to write the opinion supporting this decision. Those in the minority may either just express their dissent or may, as they more usually do, write separate opinions in which they express their reasons for disagreeing with the majority decision. These dissenting opinions do not have the force of law and cannot, therefore, be regarded as precedents for future decisions. Actually, however, it often happens that the views expressed in dissenting opinions later become accepted by the Court as being the right ones. This has been particularly true of the numerous dissenting opinions written by the late Justice Oliver Wendell Holmes. It is even possible that there may be a disagreement among those holding the majority view. In this case one or more concurring opinions may be written giving reasons for agreement with the decision that differ from those given by the principal opinion. The reasonings used in such concurring opinions, again as in the case of dissenting opinions, are not technically precedents but, practically speaking, the reasoning there used is of great weight in future cases.

SUMMARY

1. Under the Constitution of the United States educational matters are within the jurisdiction of the states rather than of the federal government.

2. Law cases involving educational questions come to the federal courts only when questions of rights under the federal Constitution are involved.

3. The provisions of the First Amendment apply to the states as well as to the federal government under the provisions of the Fourteenth Amendment as interpreted by the Supreme Court.

4. Cases of the type discussed in this book may originally be brought either in the state courts or in the federal courts.

5. The Supreme Court of the United States decides which cases it will hear and decide. Most requests for hearings are denied.

6. Courts will not decide hypothetical or moot cases where a real issue is not involved.

7. The material in this book should be read with as much care being given to noticing what the Court does *not* say as to what it *does* say.

8. When opinions contain material not directly pertinent to the case at issue this is referred to as *dictum* and does not have the same weight in setting precedents for future decisions as relevant matter does.

9. Stability in the law is maintained by the doctrine of *stare decisis* which means that courts will follow previously rendered decisions save in exceptional instances. Such instances include: (a) overruling previous decisions directly; (b) distinguishing the instant case from the precedent; and, (c) changing a decision on rehearing.

10. A long period of time elapses between the initiation of a law case and the final determination of that case by a decision of the Supreme Court of the United States.

11. Many decisions of the Supreme Court are reached by a divided Court. Often there are, in addition to the opinion of the Court, dissenting and concurring opinions.

CHAPTER 2
RELIGION AND THE SCHOOL

In a society where there is only a minimum of diversity in religious attitudes, views, and beliefs there is little or no difficulty in establishing satisfactory policies concerning religious activities in the schools. It is only when a diversity of views exists that the determination of such a policy presents a serious and sometimes painful problem. This problem is exacerbated as the degree of diversity increases.

Generally speaking, immigrants to the American colonies as well as to the United States have come from areas where there was little diversity in religious attitudes and beliefs. This was true even when groups came to America to escape religious persecution. The group coming to America in such cases was usually quite homogeneous in this respect. It came from a society in which there was a commonly accepted, if not always an officially established, religion. For example, when Jews migrated to the United States, more often than not they came from countries where there was one generally accepted Christian denomination. Usually the Jewish group was also one that was not heterodox in its religious outlook.

To live in a society marked by extreme diversity in re-

ligious beliefs was consequently a new experience for practically all immigrants to America, from the earliest colonists to
the most recent arrivals. It is, of course, true that some of the
early colonies were just as homogeneous in a religious sense as
were the European centers from which the colonists came.
Gradually, however, these colonies tended to become more
diverse in this respect. That the process of adjustment has been
a difficult one, fraught with controversy, compromise, antago-
nism, reconciliation, emotion, and reason, is not surprising.

Some adjustment can, perhaps, be facilitated by court
decisions. A spirit of tolerance and understanding and above all
a recognition of the reality of this diversity are, however, the
most necessary ingredients.

REFUSAL TO RECOGNIZE DIVERSITY

One may, perhaps, feel that there is very little understanding in the 1960s about any diversity in religious outlook.
When the situation is compared, however, with the degree of
acceptance of diverse religious views in our earlier American
history, it is obvious that we have come a long way on the road
to a satisfactory adjustment. Only a few examples are needed
to illustrate the point. Anything remotely approaching an adequate historical treatment of this complex subject will not be
attempted.

King James in chartering the Virginia Company in 1606
required that "the true word, and service of God and Christian
[italics are mine] faith be preached, planted and used . . ."

In 1649 a Toleration Act was passed in the colony of
Maryland. It guaranteed religious liberty to Trinitarian Christians but not to non-Christians.

In 1700 the Law of the Province of New York provided
that Roman Catholic priests performing religious rites or teaching Catholic doctrine should be imprisoned for life.

Maryland passed a law in 1704 prohibiting the baptism of children by Roman Catholic priests.

Fourteen years later public officials of Maryland who attended Catholic mass were subjected to severe punishments.

For a six-year period beginning in 1768, Baptists were persecuted in Virginia and were sentenced by courts to be whipped, jailed, and fined.

In 1776, the year that Americans associate with the great enduring principles of freedom, one who denied the Trinity was subject to a three-year period of imprisonment, and Unitarians and freethinkers were deprived of the custody of their children according to Virginia law.

In 1789 a Massachusetts law required participation by the clergy in public school supervision and teacher certification.

In 1834 Samuel F. B. Morse wrote a series of articles in the *New York Journal of Commerce* advocating the closing of all Roman Catholic schools.

In the same year in Charlestown, Massachusetts, a Catholic convent was burned by an anti-Catholic mob.

In 1840 the Catholic Fourth Provincial Council ordered all priests to see to it that Catholic children did not use Protestant Bibles or sing Protestant hymns in the public school.

In 1844 the Supreme Court of the United States in the case of *Vidal* v. *Girard's Executors* stated that Christianity was "part of the common law of the land."

Horace Mann, generally regarded as the "father" of the public school in America, in his final annual report as secretary of the Massachusetts Board of Education stated in 1848 that "the Bible is the acknowledged expositor of Christianity . . . This Bible is in our Common Schools by common consent."

In 1854 riots occurred and Roman Catholic property was destroyed by mob action in Ellsworth, Maryland.

In 1887 an association was formed in Iowa to fight Roman Catholic "subversion" of the public schools.

Justice Brewer in his opinion on behalf of the Supreme

Court of the United States in the case of *Church of the Holy Trinity v. United States* declared that the United States was "a Christian nation."

In 1845 the Supreme Court held that the First Amendment did not protect the American Indian from religious oppression on the part of tribal authorities. Until very recently (1934), the administrative control of the American Indian recognized no right of religious freedom.

RECOGNITION OF RELIGIOUS DIVERSITY

Not all of the events transpiring in our early history were marked by the intolerance of opposing or different religious views. The following are only a few of the many instances which might be cited.

The Rhode Island charter granted to Roger Williams in 1647 provided for complete separation of church and state.

In 1754 the royal charter granted to King's College (now Columbia University) forbade the college authorities to "exclude any person of any religious denomination whatsover from equal liberty and advantage of education, or from any of the degrees, liberties, privileges, benefits or immunities . . . on account of his particular tenets in the matter of religion."

Ten years later the charter to what is now Brown University in Providence, Rhode Island, which was then a Baptist institution, provided that "youth of all religious denominations shall and may be freely admitted to the equal advantages, emoluments, and honor of the college or university and shall receive a like, fair, generous, and equal treatment during their residence therein . . ." This view was implemented in 1770 by the then College of Rhode Island in declaring that "the children of Jews may be admitted into this institution, and entirely enjoy the freedom of their own religion, without any constraint or imposition whatsover."

James Madison's "Remonstrance," so often cited with approval in the decisions of the Supreme Court and with which we shall be dealing in succeeding chapters, was issued in 1785. In 1786 Virginia passed Thomas Jefferson's "Act for Establishing Religious Freedom," and thus disestablished the Anglican Church in that state.

In 1790 President George Washington wrote to the Hebrew Congregation, at Newport, Rhode Island, that the United States government "gives to bigotry no sanction, to persecution no assistance."

In 1796 a treaty with Tripoli stated that the "Government of the United States of America is not, in any sense, founded on the Christian religion. . . ." In the renewal of the treaty in 1805, however, this statement was omitted.

In 1833 Massachusetts disestablished the Congregational Church.

In 1840 the Governor of New York State recommended to the legislature that public schools be established in which immigrant children, "may be instructed by teachers speaking the same language with themselves and professing in the same faith."

In 1875 President Grant strongly advocated the elimination of religious and sectarian influences in the public schools, saying: "Encourage free schools and resolve that not one dollar appropriated for their support shall be appropriated to the support of any sectarian school. Resolve that neither the state nor the nation, nor both combined, shall support institutions of learning other than those sufficient to afford every child growing up in the land an opportunity of a good common school education, unmixed with sectarian, pagan, or atheistical dogmas. Leave the matter of religion to the family altar, the church, and the private school, supported entirely by private contributions. Keep the church and state forever separate." In the same year he proposed a constitutional amendment to assure that these principles be carried out. It was not adopted.

ESTABLISHMENT OF PAROCHIAL SCHOOLS

One result of the conflicting policies described in the preceding pages was the foundation of private, religious "parochial" schools. Technically, not all private, religiously sponsored schools are "parochial" schools. The use of the term to identify such schools has become so general, however, that it will be used in this manner in this book.

By 1800, for example, some 188 Dutch Reformed churches had established 144 such schools.

In 1820 it was reported that there were 206 parochial schools sponsored by 84 Lutheran congregations. By 1892 this number had increased to 380.

The first Roman Catholic parochial school was opened in Philadelphia in 1782. In 1731 the first Jewish parochial school had been established in New York City. During the quarter century after 1846, 246 parochial schools were established by the Presbyterian Church in 29 states.

GOVERNMENT AID TO RELIGIOUS SCHOOLS

There are many instances of funds being appropriated by both federal and state governments to support religiously sponsored educational institutions. Examples abound; the following are given only as illustrative and with no pretense of completeness.

In 1787, the year in which the now-famous Northwest Ordinance was passed, Congress authorized the sale of federal lands to the Ohio Company with the stipulation that one lot in each township "be given perpetually for the purposes of religion."

In 1795 New York State appropriated money for Protestant, Catholic, and Jewish denominational charity schools. This was done at least through 1801.

In 1804 the Presbyterian Ohio University received state grants.

Congress made land grants to Baptist Columbian College, now George Washington University, in 1832. In 1833 similar grants were made to Roman Catholic Georgetown College.

From 1835 to 1844 in Lowell, Massachusetts, Catholic schools received public money with the understanding that religion would be taught only after school hours.

During the six years following 1865, the Freedman's Bureau, federally financed, spent over $5 million for Negro schools, most of which were operated by religious societies.

As late as 1870 Congress appropriated the sum $10,000 to Methodist Wilberforce University.

In 1888 federal funds were provided for Presbyterian, Episcopalian, Roman Catholic and other mission schools in Alaska.

A reading of the foregoing items should certainly establish beyond any doubt that there was little uniformity or consistency in the attempted solutions to the problem of the proper relationship between religion and public education in the history of the United States.

THE SCHOOLS TODAY

A view of the situation at the present time will be helpful to an understanding of the present controversies which will be discussed shortly.

There are today in the United States about 105,000 elementary and 30,000 secondary schools operated by the several states as part of the public school system. The enrolment in these schools is estimated to be 30,125,000 and 9,600,000 respectively. There are about 14,000 elementary and 4,000 secondary schools with estimated enrolments of 5,300,000 and 1,000,-

000 respectively, operated under private auspices. The largest number of these private schools, about 10,000 elementary and 1,500 secondary, with about 4,500,000 and 600,000 pupils, respectively, are operated by the Roman Catholic Church.

There are today in the United States at least 86 religious groups with memberships of over 50,000, as well as innumerable smaller groups. A summary is given in the following table showing information taken from the *Yearbook of American Churches*.

CENSUS OF U.S. RELIGIOUS GROUPS

RELIGIOUS GROUP	NUMBER OF CHURCHES	NUMBER OF MEMBERS	NUMBER OF CLERGY
Buddhist	55	60,000	90
Old Catholic, Polish National Catholic, etc.	329	497,527	328
Eastern Churches	1,531	3,094,140	1,903
Jewish	4,079	5,585,000	5,070
Roman Catholic	23,541	44,874,371	57,616
Protestant (226 bodies)	292,233	66,854,200	332,044

Source: *Yearbook of American Churches*, 1965. National Council of the Churches of Christ in the U.S.A., New York, 1965.

The seeds of the controversy, reaching somewhat of a climax during the past two decades, can be discerned in the historical events included in this chapter. The growing diversity of religious views that has come to be a generally accepted fact of American life is also traceable in the history of our country and its population growth through immigration.

BASES FOR CONTROVERSY

There are four principal classes of controversy that concern the relationship of public schools and religion. The first concerns the propriety of expending public tax moneys for what may be deemed by some to be a religious purpose. Secondly, problems arise as to the appropriateness under the Constitution of the inclusion in public schools of activities of a religious character. A third type of problem arises in connection with the right of the public school to require participation in activities considered antithetical to the religious convictions of a pupil. The fourth class of problem concerns the right of the state to regulate activities of nonpublic schools operated and financed by religious organizations.

These problems will be discussed separately, but it is not proposed to include a complete list of issues arising under the four headings. Nor will any attempt be made to go into detail as to which states have statutes or constitutional provisions governing, or court decisions determining, these issues. To give complete information would unnecessarily lengthen this portion of the book. There will, however, be an attempt to point out areas that have been definitely adjudicated by the Supreme Court of the United States and also to call attention to the conflict among states as to policy and practice in connection with some of these items.

Expenditure of public tax money for religious purposes

1. May tax money be used to furnish textbooks to pupils attending parochial schools?

Insofar as the federal Constitution is concerned the answer appears to be "yes." The case of *Cochran* v. *Louisiana*, decided in 1930 and discussed in Chapter 5, so determined even though it made no mention of the First Amendment.

As far as the states are concerned, constitutional provisions, statutes, and policies differ. Textbooks and supplies are provided for both public and parochial school pupils in a number of states. In others there are specific constitutional and statutory provisions forbidding this, while in still others it is not done as a matter of legislative policy.

Usually, when this type of expenditure is upheld it is done on the "child-benefit" theory, which states that such an expenditure is not for the benefit of the religious organization operating the school but for the benefit of the individual child concerned.

Other expenditures which have been justified under the child-benefit theory are: (a) the furnishing of equal health services to public and private school pupils; (b) the payment of transportation expenses to such pupils. The latter expenditure is discussed at length in Chapter 5 in the treatment of the *Everson* case. A number of state courts have, however, ruled specifically that as a contribution to religious purposes such an expenditure is contrary to state constitutional provisions. Justice Douglas in his concurring opinion in the *Schempp* case, discussed in Chapter 8, stated that he doubted that the ruling in the *Everson* case which permitted such an expenditure would be allowed to stand if it was again considered by the Supreme Court. As late as 1961, though, the Supreme Court refused to consider a case raising this question which had arisen in Connecticut; (c) the federal hot lunch program specifically applied its provisions to private as well as public school pupils; (d) under the G.I. Bill veterans were permitted to attend religiously sponsored schools while receiving their benefits; (e) under the provisions of the National Defense Education Act, funds for the improvement of science, mathematics, and language teaching were made available to parochial as well as to public schools.

2. May real and personal property be exempted from taxation when used for religious purposes even when these purposes include operation of educational institutions?

An affirmative answer to this question has been universally assumed. There is language in several Supreme Court opinions to this effect but the question has never been specifically raised before the Court. State constitutional provisions and state court decisions have upheld the propriety of such exemptions.

3. May funds made available by the Federal Aid to Education law of 1965 constitutionally be distributed to the states

for the benefit of private and parochial schools as well as for public schools?

This is an undecided question. There are many proponents of both negative and affirmative answers. It is a well-known fact that the lack of certainty of the answer to this problem has had a great deal to do with the reluctance of Congress to legislate for the aid of schools. At a press conference, President Kennedy stated, no doubt on the basis of legal advice, that he felt that such a distribution was barred by the language of the *Everson* case. (See Chapter 6.) It is interesting to note that the federal legislation providing for loans and grants to colleges for building purposes, which was signed into law in December 1963, is specifically made applicable to all collegiate institutions rather than only to publicly supported ones.

4. May public school authorities rent or lease space to or from religious bodies for school purposes?

There are a number of conflicting rulings on this point by state courts. Policy also varies widely on this issue. No definite answer has ever been given by the Supreme Court as to the constitutionality of such procedures, which, incidentally, are quite widespread.

What, if any, religious activities are permissible in the public school classroom?

Prayer: The language of the Supreme Court in the *Vitale* (Chapter 7) and *Schempp* (Chapter 8) cases leaves little doubt that the recitation of a prayer in a public school classroom is a religious exercise which is prohibited by the Establishment Clause of the First Amendment. The question as to whether the daily allotment of time for a period of silent meditation falls under the proscription of these decisions is an unanswered one. May a patriotic song, for example, the fourth verse of *America*, or a historical document like the Declaration of Independence be used as a prayer? The State Department of Education of

New York State has issued a ruling that forbids this procedure. It is an open question on which policy in the several states will, no doubt, differ sharply. I know of no court decisions on this issue.

Reading of the Bible: The *Schempp* and *Murray* cases (Chapter 8) say unequivocally that the Bible may not be read in a public school classroom as a religious exercise. It seems reasonable to assume that there would be a controversy about this issue even if it were read as a literary or historical document since it has such strong religious implications to so many of the people of the United States. The situation is complicated by the existence of a number of versions of the Bible. The answer seems to lie in the manner in which the reading takes place and in the context in which it is done. It is unlikely that courts would hold invalid such reading under a set of facts showing a genuine historical or literary purpose for the reading.

Observance of religious holidays: A highly sensitive and controversial issue arises in many schools each year concerning the observation of such religious holy days as Christmas, Hanukkah, Easter, and Passover. This issue is a source of much soul-searching by school boards, administrators, and teachers. Court decisions have been at variance on the propriety of exhibiting creches, the presence in the classroom of Christmas trees and other symbols, the presentation of school programs in connection with these holidays, and in other manifestations of the observance. As we shall see in Chapter 8, this question was raised in the *Chamberlin* case and remains thus undecided insofar as the Supreme Court of the United States is concerned.

Singing of hymns and recitation of Psalms: The language of the *Schempp* decision (Chapter 8) seems broad enough to justify the statement that such activities are beyond the permissible limits set by the Establishment Clause of the First Amendment.

Recitation of the Pledge of Allegiance to the Flag including the words, "Under God": The Supreme Court ruled in

71633

LIBRARY
College of St. Francis
JOLIET, ILL.

West Virginia v. *Barnette* (Chapter 5) that children who had religious scruples against taking part in the Pledge need not take part in this exercise, but it did not bar the use of the Pledge of Allegiance in the classroom. The Supreme Court of the United States in November 1964 refused to accept jurisdiction of a New York case involving the validity from a constitutional standpoint of requiring the recitation of the Pledge including the words, "under God." The New York courts had held this unobjectionable. In effect, the Supreme Court refused to interfere with this ruling.

Display of religious symbols in the classroom: Controversy about the propriety of such displays has erupted on a number of occasions, but to date this matter has not been brought to a higher court except in the *Chamberlin* case. Here the issue was not squarely decided as can be seen from the discussion of this case in Chapter 8.

Released and dismissal time for religious instruction: Discussion of this issue will be deferred. It is dealt with thoroughly in Chapter 6.

Teachers wearing religious garb: Courts faced with this question have differed in their rulings. State statutes also differ and no federal decision has been rendered on this issue.

Taking of a religious census.

Checking on pupils' Church and Sunday school attendance by public school teachers.

Distribution of religious literature in classrooms.

Using criteria involving religion in hiring teachers: It seems reasonable to suppose that under the broad language of the *Schempp* case (Chapter 8) any of the four activities listed would be prohibited.

Teaching courses in religion or comparative religion: It seems to be a reasonable conclusion that the attitude of courts toward the constitutionality of giving such courses would depend on two factors. First, it would be necessary that they be conducted in a nonsectarian manner, and second, the educational level of the pupils would be a factor. In general, courts have indicated that they would look with favor on courses *about* religion in the school under proper circumstances. Justice Brennan, in his concurring opinion in the *Schempp* case, faces this issue squarely (p. 201) and offers the opinion that such courses would be quite constitutional.

Baccalaureate services: This is another issue which was raised and left undecided in the *Chamberlin* case. Such exercises have led to much controversy and a not inconsiderable amount of litigation. State courts have differed in their rulings and the question has never been decided by the Supreme Court.

From what kind of activities in the public school classroom may an individual be excused because of religious scruples?

Pledging allegiance to the Flag: In the cases to be discussed in Chapter 5 it is clearly established that a member of a religious sect having religious scruples against pledging allegiance to the flag need not participate.

Taking courses which deal with subjects that are repugnant to religious beliefs: Can a Christian Scientist be required to take a course in health or hygiene or biology that deals with the germ theory? Can a Roman Catholic student be required to take a biology course which teaches the theory of evolution? Can a student who is a member of the Dutch Reformed Church be required to participate in gymnasium classes which include dancing as a required activity? Can a Moslem student be required to attend classes on Fridays? Can a Mennonite student be compelled to view a film shown as part of a course?

These and similar questions have confronted state courts and a variety of rulings have resulted. No case in which any of these issues was raised has been decided by the Supreme Court.

Can a student be required to take part in ROTC activities at the college level? Apparently the answer is in the affirmative. The *Hamilton* case, which is discussed in one of the opinions quoted from in Chapter 4, seems conclusive on this point. The decision, however, turned on the point that students were not legally required to attend college. The issue presented in a case where such ROTC activities took place in a school which the student was required by law to attend would be an entirely different one.

What is the role of the state in relation to parochial schools?

Requiring all children to attend public schools: It was definitely decided in the *Pierce* case, to be discussed in the next chapter, that a state has no constitutional right to institute such a requirement.

Regulating the curriculum of the parochial school: It is within the power of the state to require inclusion of some subjects but a prohibition *against* the teaching of certain subjects apparently is not permissible under the Fourteenth Amendment. This question is discussed rather thoroughly by the Supreme Court in the *Meyer* case (Chapter 3).

Certification of teachers and maintenance of educational standards: There has been, as far as I know, no serious controversy about the state's right in these respects and it seems to be generally taken for granted that the state may act to maintain adequate standards in any school within its jurisdiction.

CLARIFICATION

We will now turn this general discussion of problems presented by the diversity of viewpoints on the role of religion in education to an examination of several specific rulings by the Supreme Court of the United States. The language used by the Court will not only shed light on the particular set of facts being dealt with, but will also tend to make clear broad principles applicable to other facts and other questions. Except for the explanatory passages inserted for a variety of purposes the attempt in the following chapters will be to let the language of the Supreme Court speak for itself.

SUMMARY

1. Controversy about the proper relationship between religion and the public school arises in direct proportion to the degree of diversity in religious views and attitudes existing in a given society.

2. In the United States such a strong diversity of views on religious matters has always been characteristic but has increased through the years.

3. Many examples can be found in the history of the United States of failure to accept religious diversity. On the other hand, many instances also can be found showing an acceptance of this diversity.

4. The increasing diversity of religious views in the United States has led to the establishment of many parochial schools.

5. Four types of problems arise in connection with the determination of the proper relationship between religion and the schools.

    a. Problems related to the propriety of the expenditure of tax moneys for what may be deemed to be a religious purpose.

    b. Problems with respect to activities in the public school classroom which may be construed as being religious in character.

    c. Problems relating to requiring activities which pupils regard as antithetical to their religious beliefs.

    d. Problems related to the proper powers of the state vis-à-vis private and parochial schools.

6. Under each of these types of problems many issues have arisen. Some of the controversies have been settled by decisions

of the Supreme Court of the United States. State constitutional provisions, state statutes, and state court decisions deal with many of these issues but often there is a lack of uniformity and therefore a variety of practices is found in the several states. Some issues are not yet resolved.

CHAPTER 3

THE CONSTITUTION AND
THE NONPUBLIC SCHOOL

THE two cases which are excerpted in this chapter deal with the right of a state to regulate and to abolish nonpublic schools. The underlying issues are religious; in the *Meyer* case the attempt was to regulate and in *Pierce* it was to eliminate schools operated under religious auspices. The principles laid down by the Court in these two cases are referred to again and again in the decisions we will examine in later chapters.

Historically, the private school and the religiously oriented school preceded the public school in America. After the public school became well established, considerable public sentiment favored making that institution universal. It was felt by the proponents of this view that such universality would foster national unity and do away with the divisiveness which they associated with nonpublic schools.

MEYER v. *STATE OF NEBRASKA*[1]

This was one of a series of five cases decided by the Supreme Court on appeals from Iowa, Nebraska, and Ohio.

[1] 262 U.S. 390. Decided June 4, 1923.

These three states had passed laws forbidding the teaching of modern languages in any school, public, private, or parochial, to any child who had not completed the eighth grade.

There were also sections in the laws of these states which required that all school subjects had to be taught in the English language. The validity of this provision was not before the Court and no ruling was therefore rendered concerning it.

THE STATUTE

The Nebraska statute (1919), which was typical of the laws passed in a number of states, read in part as follows:

Section 2.   Languages, other than the English language, may be taught as languages only after a pupil shall have attained and successfully passed the eighth grade . . .

The defendant was tried and convicted on the charge that:

. . . while an instructor in Zion Parochial School, he unlawfully taught the subject of reading in the German language to a child of ten years. . . .

After his conviction, Meyer appealed first to the Supreme Court of Nebraska and then to the Supreme Court of the United States. He contended that the statute in question was in violation of his constitutional rights and therefore invalid. The State of Nebraska supported the statute and asserted its reasonableness and constitutionality.

ARGUMENT FOR THE VALIDITY OF THE STATUTE

The proponents of the statute argued that:

The statute was a legitimate exercise of the police power of the State.

The statute forbids the teaching of foreign languages to children of tender years before such children are grounded in the English tongue. It does not forbid the use of foreign languages by persons of maturity or prevent the study of foreign languages by persons who have passed the eighth grade. It does not in any way interfere with *bona fide* religious instruction or with any legitimate religion.

The object of the legislation . . . was to create an enlightened American citizenship in sympathy with the principles and ideals of this country, and to prevent children reared in America from being trained and educated in foreign languages and foreign ideals before they have had an opportunity to learn the English language and observe American ideals. It is a well known fact that the language first learned by a child remains his mother tongue and the language of his heart. . . .

The police power itself is an attribute of sovereignty. It exists without any reservation in the Constitution. It is founded on the right of the State to protect its citizens, to provide for their welfare and progress and to insure the good of society. . . . Its application varies with the exigencies of the situation and with the progress of mankind. It is the foundation of our social system and upon it depends the security of social order, the life and health of the citizen, the comfort of existence in a thickly populated community, the enjoyment of private and social life, and the beneficial use of property. It extends to the protection of life, health, comfort and welfare of persons, protection of property and to the welfare of the State itself. All natural persons within the jurisdiction hold their property and pursue their various callings subject to the police power. It is inherent in the various States of the Union, as well as in the Federal Government. To the extent that property or business is devoted to public use or is affected with a public interest it is subject to regulation by the police power. It extends to the regulation of education as the very existence of our government, as well as its progress and development, depends upon the intelligence of our citizenry. . . .

ARGUMENT AGAINST THE VALIDITY OF THE STATUTE

On the other hand, those attacking the validity of the statute, argued that:

The right to choose and pursue a given legitimate vocation is within the rights guaranteed by the Fourteenth Amendment.

The vocation of the plaintiff is teaching—a legitimate vocation—and in teaching, as he did, a certain subject in a language other than English, he encroached upon the rights of no other person. . . .

Imparting knowledge in a foreign language is not inherently immoral or inimical to the public welfare, and not a legitimate subject for prohibitory legislation. In fact, an examination of the statute will show that the legislature did not regard the teaching of a pupil in some language other than English as vicious or inimical to the public welfare. It applies only to schools, leaving teachers and others at liberty to teach privately.

When the legislature by clear implication finds that the practice or pursuit against which the act is leveled does not of itself injuriously affect the public, a measure designed to prohibit it is unconstitutional. It being clear, therefore, both upon reason and legislative finding, that the prohibited acts are not harmful, this measure, insofar as it imposes upon teachers, . . . , penalties . . . for the giving of instruction in languages, is violative of the constitutional right to engage in the practice of their chosen profession or calling. . . .

The statute, as construed by the Supreme Court of Nebraska, is prohibitive, not regulatory of a legitimate vocation.

. . . The exercise of the police power can be justified only when it adds, in a substantial way, to the security of fundamental rights.

The relation to the common good of a law fixing a minimum of education is readily perceived, but how one fixing a maximum—limiting the field of human knowledge—can serve the public welfare or add substantially to the security of life, liberty, or the pursuit of happiness is inconceivable. . . .

One claim put forward is, that the statute forwards the work of Americanization. But in our desire for the Americanization of our foreign born population we should not overlook the fact that the spirit of America is liberty and toleration. . . .

The law, . . . operates to deny the plaintiff in error the equal protection of the law.

RULING OF THE NEBRASKA
STATE SUPREME COURT

The Supreme Court of Nebraska had sustained the validity of the statute, saying in part:

The salutary purpose of the statute is clear. The legislature has seen the baneful effects of permitting foreigners, who had taken residence in this country, to rear and educate their children in the language of their native land. The result of that condition was found to be inimical to our own safety. To allow the children of foreigners, who had emigrated here, to be taught from early childhood the language of the country of their parents was to rear them with that language as their mother tongue. It was to educate them so that they must always think in that language, and, as a consequence, naturally inculcate in them the ideas and sentiments foreign to the best interests of this country. The statute, therefore, was intended not only to require that the education of all children be conducted in the English language, but that, until they had grown into that language and until it had become part of them, they should not in the schools be taught any other language. The obvious purpose of this statute was that the English language should be and become the mother tongue of all children reared in this state. The enactment comes reasonably within the police power of the state. . . .

It is suggested that the law is an unwarranted restriction, in that it applies to all citizens of the state and arbitrarily interferes with the rights of citizens who are not of foreign ancestry, and prevents them, without reason, from having their children taught foreign languages in school. The argument is not well taken, for it assumes that every citizen finds himself restrained by the statute. The hours which a child is able to devote to study in the confinement of school are limited. . . . A selection of subjects for its education, therefore, is obviously necessary. The legislature no doubt had in mind the practical operation of the law. The law affects few citizens, except those of foreign lineage. Other citizens, in their selection of studies, except perhaps in rare instances, have never deemed it of importance to teach their children foreign languages before such children have reached the eighth grade. In the legislative mind, the salutary effects of the statute no doubt outweighed the restriction upon the citizens generally, which, it appears, was a restriction of no real consequence.

DECISION OF THE UNITED STATES SUPREME COURT

The United States Supreme Court reversed the decision by a majority of 7 to 2. The opinion of the Court was delivered by Justice McReynolds and was concurred in by Chief Justice Taft, Justices McKenna, Van Devanter, Brandeis, Butler, and Sanford. The dissenting opinion was written by Justice Holmes and was concurred in by Justice Sutherland.

The Court defined the problem as follows:

The problem for our determination is whether the statute as construed and applied unreasonably infringes the liberty guaranteed to the plaintiff in error by the Fourteenth Amendment. "No State shall . . . deprive any person of life, liberty, or property, without due process of law."

THE MAJORITY OPINION

This statement was followed by a discussion of the "liberty" granted by the terms of the Fourteenth Amendment:

While this Court has not attempted to define with exactness the liberty thus guaranteed, the term has received much consideration and some of the included things have been definitely stated. Without doubt, it denotes not merely freedom from bodily restraint but also the right of the individual to contract, to engage in any of the common occupations of life, to acquire useful knowledge, to marry, establish a home and bring up children, to worship God according to the dictates of his own conscience, and generally to enjoy those privileges long recognized at common law as essential to the orderly pursuit of happiness by free men. . . . The established doctrine is that this liberty may not be interfered with, under the guise of protecting the public interest, by legislative action which is arbitrary or without reasonable relation to some purpose within the competency of the State to effect. Determination by the legislature of what constitutes proper exercise of police power is not final or conclusive but is subject to supervision by the courts. . . .

The importance of education in the American scheme is emphasized: The American people have always regarded education and acquisition of knowledge as matters of supreme importance . . . Corresponding to the right of control it is the natural duty of the parent to give his children education suitable to their station in life; and nearly all the States, including Nebraska, enforce this obligation by compulsory laws.

Practically, education of the young is only possible in schools conducted by specially qualified persons who devote themselves thereto. The calling always has been regarded as useful and honorable, essential, indeed, to the public welfare.

The Court discusses the purposes sought to be accomplished by the legislation and concludes that this end cannot be attained by illegal means:

Mere knowledge of the German language cannot reasonably be regarded as harmful. Heretofore it has been commonly looked upon as helpful and desirable. Plaintiff in error taught this language in school as part of his occupation. His right thus to teach and the right of parents to engage him so to instruct their children, we think, are within the liberty of the Amendment.

The challenged statute forbids the teaching in school of any subject except in English; also the teaching of any other language until the child has attained and successfully passed the eighth grade, which is not usually accomplished before the age of twelve. The Supreme Court of the State has held that "the so-called ancient or dead languages" are not "within the spirit or the purpose of the act." . . . Latin, Greek, Hebrew are not proscribed; but German, French, Spanish and every other alien speech are within the ban. Evidently the legislature has attempted materially to interfere with the calling of modern language teachers, with the opportunities of pupils to acquire knowledge, and with the power of parents to control the education of their own children.

It is said that the purpose of the legislation was to promote civic development by inhibiting training and education of the immature in foreign tongues and ideals before they could learn English and acquire American ideals; and "that the English language should be and become the mother tongue of all children reared in this State." . . .

That the State may do much, go very far, indeed, in order to improve the quality of its citizens, physically, mentally and morally, is clear; but the individual has certain fundamental rights which must be respected. The protection of the Constitution extends to all, to those who speak other languages as well as those born with English on the tongue. Perhaps it would be highly advantageous if all had ready understanding of our ordinary speech, but this cannot be coerced by methods which conflict with the Constitution—a desirable end cannot be promoted by prohibited means.

The desire of the legislature to foster a homogeneous people with American ideals prepared readily to understand current discussions of civic matters is easy to appreciate. Unfortunate experiences during the late war and aversion toward every characteristic of truculent adversaries were certainly enough to quicken that aspiration. But the means adopted, we think, exceed the limitations upon the power of the State and conflict with rights assured to the plaintiff in error. The interference is plain enough and no adequate reason therefor in time of peace and domestic tranquility has been shown.

The Court makes it clear that reasonable regulations for all schools are within the power of the state and that the prescription of curricula in schools supported by the state, i.e. public schools, is also a proper exercise of state authority:

The power of the State to compel attendance at some school and to make reasonable regulations for all schools, including a requirement that they shall give instruction in English, is not questioned. Nor has challenge been made of the State's power to prescribe a curriculum for institutions which it supports. Those matters are not within the present controversy. Our concern is with the prohibition approved by the Supreme Court. . . . mere abuse incident to an occupation ordinarily useful is not enough to justify its abolition, although regulation may be entirely proper. . . . We are constrained to conclude that the statute as applied is arbitrary and without reasonable relation to any end within the competency of the State.

The judgment of the court below must be reversed. . . .

THE DISSENTING OPINION

Justice Holmes in his brief dissent said:

We all agree, I take it, that it is desirable that all the citizens of the United States should speak a common tongue, and therefore that the end aimed at by the statute is a lawful and proper one. The only question is whether the means adopted deprive teachers of the liberty secured to them by the Fourteenth Amendment. . . . I cannot bring my mind to believe that in some circumstances, and circumstances existing it is said, in Nebraska, the statute might not be regarded as a reasonable or even necessary method of reaching the desired result. The part of the act with which we are concerned deals with the teaching of young children. Youth is the time when familiarity with a language is established and if there are sections in the State where a child would hear only Polish or French or German spoken at home I am not prepared to say that it is unreasonable to provide that in his early years he shall hear and speak only English at school. But if it is reasonable it is not an undue restriction of the liberty either of teacher or scholar. No one would doubt that a teacher might be forbidden to teach many things, and the only criterion of his liberty under the Constitution that I can think of is whether, considering the end in view, the statute passes the bounds of reason and assumes the character of a merely arbitrary fiat. . . . I think that I appreciate the objection to the law but it appears to me to present a question upon which men reasonably might differ and therefore I am unable to say that the Constitution of the United States prevents the experiment being tried.

The decision in *Meyer* v. *Nebraska* was that a statute proscribing the teaching below the ninth grade level of modern foreign languages in private schools was in violation of the Due Process Clause of the Fourteenth Amendment. The argument that such a regulation fell within the proper police powers of a state was rejected.

PIERCE, GOVERNOR OF OREGON et al. v. SOCIETY OF SISTERS et al.[2]

The question presented to the Supreme Court in this case was whether or not a state statute requiring all children to attend public rather than private schools was valid under the provisions of the Due Process Clause of the Fourteenth Amendment.

THE STATUTE

In November 1922 the voters of the State of Oregon passed an initiative act to be effective in September 1926, which read in part as follows:

Children Between the Ages of Eight and Sixteen Years—Any parent, guardian or other person in the State of Oregon, having control or charge or custody of a child under the age of sixteen years and of the age of eight years or over . . . who shall fail or neglect or refuse to send such a child to a public school for the period of time a public school shall be held during the current year in said district, shall be guilty of a misdemeanor . . . provided, that in the following cases, children shall not be required to attend public schools:
(a) *Children Physically Unable—* . . .
(b) *Children Who Have Completed the Eighth Grade—* . . .
(c) *Distance from School—* . . .
(d) *Private Instruction*—Any child who is being taught for a like period of time by the parent or private teacher such subjects as are usually taught in the first eight years in the public school; but before such child can be taught by a parent or a private teacher, such parent or private teacher must receive written permission from the county superintendent, . . .

2 268 U.S. 510. Decided June 1, 1925.

Penalties were provided for violation of the act.

An action to bar enforcement of this act was brought by the Society of Sisters of the Holy Names of Jesus and Mary and by the Hill Military Academy.

THE SOCIETY OF SISTERS

The Society of Sisters was described by the Supreme Court as follows:

. . . The Society of Sisters, is an Oregon corporation, organized in 1880, with power to care for orphans, educate and instruct the youth, establish and maintain academies and schools, and acquire necessary real and personal property. It has long devoted its property and effort to the secular and religious education and care of children, . . . It conducts interdependent primary and high schools and junior colleges and maintains orphanages . . . In its primary schools many children . . . are taught the subjects usually pursued in Oregon public schools during the first eight years. Systematic religious instruction and moral training according to tenets of the Roman Catholic Church are also regularly provided. All courses of study, both temporal and religious, contemplate continuity of training under appellee's charge; the primary schools are essential to the system and the most profitable. It owns valuable buildings, especially constructed and equipped for school purposes. The business is remunerative—the annual income from primary schools exceeds thirty thousand dollars—and the successful conduct of this requires long time contracts with teachers and parents. The Compulsory Education Act of 1922 has already caused the withdrawal from its schools of children who would otherwise continue, and their income has steadily declined.

THE HILL MILITARY ACADEMY

The Court said of the Hill Military Academy:

. . . Hill Military Academy, is a private corporation organized in 1908 . . . engaged in owning, operating, and conducting for profit an elementary, college preparatory and military training school for boys between the ages of five and twenty-one years. The average attendance is one hundred and the annual fees received for each student amount to some eight hundred dollars. The elementary department is divided into eight grades, as in the public schools; the college preparatory department has four grades, similar to those of the public high schools; the courses of study conform to the requirements of the State Board of Education. Military instruction and training are also given, . . . It owns considerable real and personal property, some useful only for school purposes. . . . In order to conduct its affairs long time contracts must be made for supplies, equipment, teachers and pupils. Appellants, law officers of the State and County, have publicly announced that the Act of November 7, 1922, is valid and have declared their intention to enforce it. By reason of the statute and threat of enforcement appellee's business is being destroyed and its property depreciated; parents and guardians are refusing to make contracts for the future instruction of their sons, and some are being withdrawn.

The Academy's bill states the foregoing facts and then alleges that the challenged Act contravenes the corporation's rights guaranteed by the Fourteenth Amendment and that unless appellants are restrained from proclaiming its validity and threatening to enforce it irreparable injury will result. The prayer is for an appropriate injunction.

DECISION OF THE TRIAL COURT

The case was first decided by a three-judge Federal District Court in March 1924. That court ruled unanimously that the enforcement of the law should be enjoined as being violative of the provisions of the Fourteenth Amendment. The lower court stated:

Complainants' right to carry on their schools, whether parochial or private, is a property right. . . . and the right of parents and guardians to send their children . . . to such schools as they may desire is not in conflict with lawful requirements but is a privilege they inherently are entitled to enjoy.

Stating that a state's police power cannot be exercised arbitrarily, they continue:

The absolute right of these schools to teach in the grammar grades . . . and the right of the parents to engage them to instruct their children, we think, is within the liberty of the Fourteenth Amendment.

The lower court relied strongly on *Meyer v. Nebraska.*

ARGUMENT THAT THE STATUTE IS UNCONSTITUTIONAL

When the case came to the United States Supreme Court for decision, the original plaintiffs argued that:

The enactment in suit is not a legitimate exercise of the police power of the State. The courts are entrusted with authority, and it becomes their solemn duty, to review the reasonableness and propriety of any attempted use of that power. . . . This Court, like the court below, must know that the true purpose of the act, as well as its plain and intended practical effect, was the destruction of private primary, preparatory and parochial schools; for they certainly could not survive the denial of the right of parents to have their children thus educated in the primary grades. . . . Private and religious schools have existed in this country from the earliest times. . . . Perhaps no institution is older or a more intimate part of our colonial and national life than religious schools and colleges, both Catholic and Protestant. . . . Out of them have developed our greatest colleges and universities, the most important of them to this day being private or religious institutions. . . . The legislation before the court manifestly carries within itself a threat, not merely to the private elementary and preparatory schools which it now practically proscribes, but to every private or religious college or university in the land. The statute in suit is so unusual and extraordinary that it must arouse misgivings in the judicial mind upon even the slightest reflection. More than ever must it be borne in mind in judging it, . . . , that "restraints must not be arbitrary or unreasonable." Freedom is the general rule, and restraint the exception.

The statute abridges the freedom of four classes closely inter-related: (1) the freedom of the private and parochial schools, (2) the freedom of teachers engaged in those schools, (3) the freedom of parents and guardians, and (4) the freedom of children. There is nothing in the record which warrants even the suggestion that private and parochial schools in Oregon are in any respect inferior to the public schools. . . . The State of Oregon has regulatory power adequate to every reasonable and proper need in this rela-tion. . . .

Where regulation is so completely adequate, prohibition is un-necessary and constitutes mere arbitrariness and wanton abuse of power. Particularly must this be true, where the subject of the alleged prohibition is an ordinary, innocuous and useful calling, trade, or business. . . .

That the assimilation of the foreigner is not a justification for any such prohibitory statute, was expressly decided in *Meyer v. Nebraska*. But the fact is, that the whole contention is fallacious and merely a far-fetched extravagance or pretense. Oregon has no substantial unnaturalized immigrant problem. Eighty-five per cent of its population is native-born. Half of the remainder is naturalized and presumably Americanized. Of the children of the seven and a half per cent unnaturalized, only a small number attend private schools. . . . The public school is not a "melting pot." Schools are, and obviously must be, located in given districts. If the neigh-borhood be American, the school there will have a similar character. If, however, it be situated in a poor and foreign quarter, the school will be attended almost entirely by children of the poorer class of foreigners. The child of a foreigner is quite as likely to be assimilated and Americanized in a private or parochial school as in a public school. . . . The private and parochial schools teach the same sub-jects as the public schools—whatever one does to inculcate and foster patriotism, the other can and does do quite as well.

No legislation can proscribe social discrimination, and the statute in the case at bar is singularly inappropriate to that end. Young children do not discriminate against each other; that is characteristic of maturity. The picking and choosing of friends for reasons based upon money, creed, or social status come, not during elementary school days, but afterwards; and no force thus far vouchsafed to man has ever been equal to the destruction or elimination of social distinctions. How the act in suit could accomplish that result, no one can tell; and, as a reason for annihilating the appellee's useful and honorable business, it amounts to nothing. It is now intimated that the statute was necessary in order to effectuate compulsory education. But the suggestion is clearly based upon false premises. The notion that private and public schools cannot exist in peace and harmony side by side, . . . is not only contradicted by long experience, but is probably held by no competent educator.

Thus far we have considered the enactment in suit only with reference to the rights of the private and parochial schools and the teachers they employ. But there is involved in the case at bar a far more important group of individual rights, namely, the rights of the parents and guardians who desire to send their children to such schools, and the rights of the children themselves. Reflection should soon convince the court that those rights which the statute seriously abridges and impairs, are of the very essence of personal liberty and freedom. . . . It is not seriously debatable that the parental right to guide one's child intellectually and religiously is a most substantial part of the liberty and freedom of the parent.

The statute in suit trespasses, not only upon the liberty of the parents individually, but upon their liberty collectively as well. It forbids them, as a body, to support private and parochial schools and thus give to their children such education and religious training as the parents may see fit, subject to the valid regulations of the State. In whatever light the act in suit be regarded, it must be manifest that, in the end, it embodies the pernicious policy of state monopoly of education.

The legislative power of a State in relation to education does not involve the power to prohibit or suppress private schools and colleges. The familiar statement that education is a public function means no more than that it is a function that the State may undertake, because it vitally interests and concerns the State that children shall be furnished the means of education and not left to grow up in ignorance. But the power of the State to provide public schools carries with it no power to prohibit and suppress private schools and colleges which are competent and qualified to afford what the State wants, namely education. . . .

ARGUMENT SUPPORTING THE CONSTITUTIONALITY OF THE STATUTE

Those seeking to uphold the validity of the legislation argued in part as follows:

Even in the freest country no person can possess absolutely uncontrolled liberty, either with respect to himself personally, or to his children. A parent cannot have a more complete right of control over the actions of his child than over his own actions. Liberty of all is subject to reasonable conditions deemed essential by the governing body to the safety, health, peace, good order and morals of the community. . . .

Under all governments, even those which are the most free and democratic in their character, the citizen must always owe duties to the State; and it necessarily follows that the State has an interest in making it certain . . . that the citizen is fitted, both in mind and body, to perform these duties. . . . The discretionary powers of a State are broad enough to permit it to decide that compulsory attendance at public schools is a proper "precautionary measure against the moral pestilence of paupers, vagabonds, and possibly convicts." . . .

. . . In this connection, it should be remembered that the vast majority of children not now attending the public schools of Oregon who will be compelled to do so by the new statute, are either themselves immigrants or the children of immigrants. Surely a State can require of all immigrants admitted to the advantages and opportunities of life in the United States, that their children shall be taught by the State the English language and the character of American institutions and government. . . .

The compulsory attendance of all children of school age at the public schools during the relatively short hours during which the schools are in session would not deprive the parents of any just rights. There would remain an abundance of time and opportunity for supplementary instruction either in religion or in the language, history, and traditions of the land of their ancestors. The objectional feature about the Nebraska law was that it forbade the teaching of modern languages either in regular schools or in supplementary schools. . . .

The discretion of the States in the exercise of their powers is broad enough to justify a State in holding that a compulsory system of public school education will encourage the patriotism of its citizens, and train its younger citizens to become more willing and more efficient defenders of the United States in times of public danger. If a State cannot compel certain children to attend public schools it cannot compel any children to do so. An attempt to do so would be clearly a violation of the "equal protection of the laws" clause of the Fourteenth Amendment.

The statute does not interfere with religious liberty. The American people as a whole have unalterably determined that there shall be an absolute and unequivocal separation of church and state, and that the public schools shall be maintained and conducted free from influences in favor of any religious organization, sect, creed or belief.

THE UNANIMOUS OPINION OF THE SUPREME COURT

The decision of the Court in favor of those seeking to restrain the enforcement of this law was unanimous. The opinion was delivered by Justice McReynolds. After describing the nature of the suit, the Court stated in referring to the legislation in question:

The manifest purpose is to compel general attendance at public schools by normal children, between eight and sixteen, who have not completed the eighth grade.

After disposing of certain technical points which were at issue, the Court reaches the main question and says:

No question is raised concerning the power of the State reasonably to regulate all schools, to inspect, supervise and examine them, their teachers and pupils; to require that all children of proper age attend some school, that teachers shall be of good moral character and patriotic disposition, that certain studies plainly essential to good citizenship be taught, and that nothing be taught which is manifestly inimical to the public welfare.

The inevitable practical result of enforcing the Act under consideration would be destruction of appellee's primary schools, and perhaps all other private primary schools for normal children in the State of Oregon. These parties are engaged in a kind of undertaking not inherently harmful, but long regarded as useful and meritorious. Certainly there is nothing in the present records to indicate that they have failed to discharge their obligations to patrons, students or the State. And there are no peculiar circumstances or present emergencies which demand extraordinary measures relative to primary education.

Under the doctrine of *Meyer* v. *Nebraska*, we think it entirely plain that the Act . . . unreasonably interferes with the liberty of parents and guardians to direct the upbringing and education of children under their control. As often heretofore pointed out, rights guaranteed by the Constitution may not be abridged by legislation which has no reasonable relation to some purpose within the competency of the State. The fundamental theory of liberty upon which all governments in this Union repose excludes any general power of the State to standardize its children by forcing them to accept instruction from public teachers only. The child is not the mere creature of the State; those who nurture him and direct his destiny have the right, coupled with the high duty, to recognize and prepare him for additional obligations.

It must be noted that in neither the *Pierce* nor the *Meyer* case was mention made of the First Amendment. Yet we will find in examining later cases involving the Establishment and Free Exercise clauses of the First Amendment that great stress is laid on the doctrine set forth in these cases.

Thus, it was decided in *Pierce* v. *Society of Sisters* that a state requirement to the effect that all children of school age must attend public schools, thus depriving them and their parents of the right to avail themselves of private schools, was in violation of the Due Process Clause of the Fourteenth Amendment.

SUMMARY

1. The private and religiously oriented school preceded the public school in America.

2. In the 1920s considerable public sentiment favored greater control over private schools and even the universality of the public school.

3. In a number of states laws were passed forbidding the teaching of foreign languages in the elementary school.

4. In *Meyer v. State of Nebraska* such a statute was challenged on the ground that it deprived parents and teachers of their liberty in contravention of the Fourteenth Amendment. The statutes were defended as a proper exercise of the states' police powers.

5. The Nebraska Supreme Court upheld the statute on the ground that it would have the effect of Americanizing foreigners.

6. The Supreme Court of the United States reversed that decision on the ground that the prohibition was an unreasonable deprivation of liberty.

7. Two Justices dissented on the ground that the statute was a reasonable regulation.

8. In Oregon the people passed an initiative measure in 1922 which provided that all elementary school age children were compelled to attend public schools.

9. The validity of this law was challenged by a Catholic school and a private military academy under the terms of the Fourteenth Amendment as a deprivation of a property right.

10. In *Pierce v. Society of Sisters* the Supreme Court affirmed a lower federal court ruling that the law interfered with rights granted by the Constitution and was not the type of reasonable regulation of private education that lies within the power of the state.

11. The First Amendment was not referred to either in the argument of counsel or in the decision in either of these two cases but, nevertheless, these cases are relied upon in later cases dealing with First Amendment issues.

CHAPTER 4
COMPULSORY FLAG SALUTE

THE two cases in this chapter are important for several reasons. The opinions were the first to make a thorough and searching examination of the problems raised by the freedom of religion guarantees of the First Amendment in its relationship to educational and school matters.

Although the first of these cases, *Minersville v. Gobitis* was decided by an 8-to-1 majority in June of 1940, this precedent was overruled in *Board of Education v. Barnette* just three years later in June of 1943. While the overruling of a previous decision is not unprecedented, it is a relatively rare event as the Supreme Court has tended to distinguish the facts in one case from another rather than to overrule a prior decision. Another factor that renders this situation unusual is that the personnel on the Court was almost the same at the time of the two decisions.

MINERSVILLE SCHOOL DISTRICT, BOARD OF EDUCATION OF MINERSVILLE SCHOOL DISTRICT et al. v. GOBITIS et al.[1]

The issue in this case was whether a requirement that all children participate in the daily flag salute in the public school classroom was in violation of the First Amendment's Free Exer-

[1] 310 U.S. 586. Decided June 3, 1940.

cise Clause insofar as children who had religious scruples against participating were concerned.

Both the United States District Court and the Circuit Court of Appeals had ruled in favor of the plaintiffs but these rulings were reversed by the Supreme Court, which had previously refused to accept jurisdiction in three cases involving almost identical facts on the ground that no federal question was involved.

On November 6, 1935, the School Board of Minersville, Pennsylvania, adopted a school regulation requiring all teachers and pupils of the schools to salute the American flag as part of the daily exercises and providing that refusal to salute the flag should be regarded as an act of insubordination.

On that day the two Gobitis children, aged 10 and 12, refused to obey the regulation on the ground that to do so would be against their religious convictions as members of Jehovah's Witnesses. They were expelled from school and had attended private schools from that time until the Supreme Court decision four and a half years later.

ARGUMENT IN FAVOR OF THE REGULATION

The school district argued that:

The refusal of the children to salute the national flag at school exercises because they believed that to do so would violate the written law of Almighty God as contained in the Bible was not founded on a religious belief. . . .

The act of saluting the flag has no bearing on what a pupil may think of his Creator. Nor is a pupil required to exhibit his religious sentiments in a particular "form of worship" when saluting the flag, because the ceremony is not, by any stretch of the imagination, a "form of worship." Like the study of history or civics or the doing of any other act which might make a pupil more patriotic as well as teach him or her "loyalty to the State and National Government," the salute has no religious implications. . . . The commandments of Jehovah, as set forth in the Bible, do not prohibit the saluting of a national flag but on the contrary approve of that practice.

The act of saluting the flag is only one of many ways in which a citizen may evidence his respect for the Government. The same respect is shown the American flag when it passes in a parade; yet that is not a religious rite.

Though members of Jehovah's Witnesses endeavor to extend religious implications to a ceremony purely patriotic in design, they do not accord to others the religious freedom which they demand for themselves, claiming that there is no limit to which they may go when they think they are worshipping God. . . .

The act of saluting the flag does not prevent a pupil, no matter what his religious belief may be, from acknowledging the spiritual sovereignty of Almighty God by rendering to God the things that are God's. . . .

ARGUMENT AGAINST THE VALIDITY OF THE REGULATION

On behalf of the Gobitis children it was argued that:

The rule compelling respondents to participate in the ceremony of saluting the flag and the act of its School Board in expelling them because they refrained, violate their rights guaranteed by . . . the Fourteenth Amendment of the Constitution of the United States.

The vital question is: Shall man be free to exercise his conscientious belief in God and his obedience to the law of Almighty God, or shall man be compelled to obey the law or the State, which law, as the creature conscientiously believes, is in direct conflict with the law of Almighty God?

This Court has repeatedly held that the individual alone is privileged to determine what he shall or shall not believe. The law, therefore, does not attempt to settle differences of creeds and confessions, or to say that any point or doctrine is too absurd to be believed. . . .

Will any court attempt to say that respondents mistakingly believe what is set forth in the twentieth chapter of Exodus in the Bible? The belief of the respondents is not based on conjecture or myth. Respondent's belief is based strictly on the Bible.

The saluting of the flag of any earthly government by a person who has covenanted to do the will of God is a form of religion and constitutes idolatry.

The rule certainly abridges the privileges of the respondents and deprives them of liberty and property without due process of law.[2]

Petitioners claim that the purpose of saluting the flag is to "Instill in the children patriotism and love of country." But why limit that compulsory rule to teachers and pupils of the public schools?

OPINION OF THE SUPREME COURT

The opinion of the Court was delivered by Justice Frankfurter and was concurred in by Chief Justice Hughes and Justices Roberts, Black, Reed, Douglas, Murphy, and McReynolds. The dissenting opinion was written by Justice Stone.

The opinion began by stating the gravity of the issue involved:

A grave responsibility confronts this Court whenever in course of litigation it must reconcile the conflicting claims of liberty and authority. But when the liberty invoked is liberty of conscience, and the authority is authority to safeguard the nation's fellowship, judicial conscience is put to its severest test.

We must decide whether the requirement of participation in such a ceremony, exacted from a child who refuses upon sincere religious grounds, infringes without due process of law the liberty guaranteed by the Fourteenth Amendment.

The nature of religious freedom next is dealt with:

Centuries of strife over the erection of particular dogmas as exclusive or all-comprehending faiths led to the inclusion of a guarantee for religious freedom in the Bill of Rights. The First Amendment, and the Fourteenth through its absorption of the First, sought to guard against repetition of those bitter religious struggles by prohibiting the establishment of a state religion and by securing to every sect the free exercise of its faith. So pervasive

[2] Cf. *Pierce* v. *Society of Sisters.*

is the acceptance of this precious right that its scope is brought into question, as here, only when the conscience of the individual collides with the felt necessities of society.

Certainly the affirmative pursuit of one's convictions about the ultimate mystery of the universe and man's relation to it is placed beyond the reach of law. Government may not interfere with organized or individual expression of belief or disbelief. Propagation of belief—or even disbelief—in the supernatural is protected, whether in church or chapel, mosque or synagogue, tabernacle or meeting-house. Likewise the Constitution assures generous immunity to the individual from imposition of penalties for offending, in the course of his own religious activities, the religious views of others, be they a minority or those who are dominant in government.

But the manifold character of man's relations may bring his conception of religious duty into conflict with the secular interests of his fellow-men. When does the constitutional guarantee compel exemption from doing what society thinks necessary for the promotion of some great common end, or from a penalty for conduct which appears dangerous to the general good? To state the problem is to recall the truth that no single principle can answer all of life's complexities. The right to freedom of religious belief, however dissident and however obnoxious to the cherished beliefs of others —even of a majority—is itself the denial of an absolute. But to affirm that the freedom to follow conscience has itself no limits in the life of a society would deny that very plurality of principles which, as a matter of history, underlies protection of religious toleration. . . . Our present task, then, as so often the case with courts, is to reconcile two rights in order to prevent either from destroying the other. . . .

In the judicial enforcement of religious freedom we are concerned with a historic concept. . . . The religious liberty which the Constitution protects has never excluded legislation of general scope not directed against doctrinal loyalties of particular sects. Judicial nullification of legislation cannot be justified by attributing to the framers of the Bill of Rights views for which there is no historic warrant. Conscientious scruples have not, in the course of the long

struggle for religious toleration, relieved the individual from obedience to a general law not aimed at the promotion or restriction of
religious beliefs. . . . The necessity for this adjustment has again
and again been recognized. . . . Nor does the freedom of speech
assured by Due Process move in a more absolute circle of immunity
than that enjoyed by religious freedom. Even if it were assumed that
freedom of speech goes beyond the historic concept of full opportunity to utter and to disseminate views, however heretical or offensive
to dominant opinion, and includes freedom from conveying what
may be deemed an implied but rejected affirmation, the question
remains whether school children, like the Gobitis children, must be
excused from conduct required of all the other children in the
promotion of national cohesion. We are dealing with an interest
inferior to none in the hierarchy of legal values. National unity is
the basis of national security. To deny the legislature the right to
select appropriate means for its attainment presents a totally different order of problem from that of the propriety of subordinating
the possible ugliness of littered streets to the free expression of
opinion through distribution of handbills. . . .

The dilemma involved in reaching a decision is described:

Situations like the present are phases of the profoundest problem
confronting a democracy—the problem which Lincoln cast in
memorable dilemma: "Must a government of necessity be too
strong for the liberties of its people, or too weak to maintain its own
existence?" . . . And when the issue demands judicial determination, it is not the personal notion of judges of what wise adjustment
requires which must prevail.

The legislative and judicial functions are discussed in the
following passage from Justice Frankfurter's opinion:

Unlike the instances we have cited, the case before us is not concerned with an exertion of legislative power for the promotion of
some specific need or interest of secular society—the protection of
the family, the promotion of health, the common defense, the
raising of public revenues to defray the cost of government. But all

these specific activities of government presuppose the existence of
an organized political society. The ultimate foundation of a free
society is the binding tie of cohesive sentiment. Such a sentiment
is fostered by all those agencies of the mind and spirit which may
serve to gather up the traditions of a people, transmit them from
generation to generation, and thereby create that continuity of a
treasured common life which constitutes a civilization. "We live
by symbols." The flag is the symbol of our national unity, transcend-
ing all internal differences, however large, within the framework
of the Constitution. This Court has had occasion to say that
". . . the flag is the symbol of the Nation's power, the emblem of
freedom in its truest, best sense. . . . it signified government rest-
ing on the consent of the governed; liberty regulated by law; the
protection of the weak against the strong; security against the
exercise of arbitrary power; and absolute safety for free institutions
against foreign aggression." . . .

The case before us must be viewed as though the legislature of
Pennsylvania had itself formally directed the flag-salute for the
children of Minersville; had made no exemption for children whose
parents were possessed of conscientious scruples like those of the
Gobitis family; and had indicated its belief in the desirable ends to
be secured by having its public school children share a common
experience at those periods of development when their minds are
supposedly receptive to its assimilation, by an exercise appropriate
in time and place and setting, and one designed to evoke in them
appreciation of the nation's hopes and dreams, its sufferings and
sacrifices. The precise issue, then, for us to decide is whether the
legislatures of the various states and the authorities in a thousand
counties and school districts of this country are barred from determining the appropriateness of various means to evoke that unifying
sentiment without which there can ultimately be no liberties, civil
or religious. To stigmatize legislative judgment in providing for this
universal gesture of respect for the symbol of our national life in the
setting of the common school as a lawless inroad on that freedom
of conscience which the Constitution protects, would amount to no
less than the pronouncement of pedagogical and psychological
dogma in a field where courts possess no marked and certainly no
controlling competence. The influences which help toward a com-

mon feeling for the common country are manifold. Some may seem harsh and others no doubt are foolish. Surely, however, the end is legitimate. And the effective means for its attainment are still so uncertain and so unauthenticated by science as to preclude us from putting the widely prevalent belief in flag-saluting beyond the pale of legislative power. . . .

The wisdom of training children in patriotic impulses by those compulsions which necessarily pervade so much of the educational process is not for our independent judgment. Even were we convinced of the folly of such a measure, such belief would be no proof of its unconstitutionality. For ourselves, we might be tempted to say that the deepest patriotism is best engendered by giving unfettered scope to the most crochety beliefs. Perhaps it is best, even from the standpoint of those interests which ordinances like the one under review seek to promote, to give the least popular sect leave from conformities like those here in issue. But the courtroom is not the arena for debating issues of educational policy. It is not our province to choose among competing considerations in the subtle process of securing effective loyalty to the traditional ideals of democracy, while respecting at the same time individual idiosyncrasies among a people so diversified in racial origins and religious allegiances. So to hold would in effect make us the school board for the country. That authority has not been given to this Court, nor should we assume it.

The educational aspects of the conflict are reviewed:

We are dealing here with the formative period in the development of citizenship. Great diversity of psychological and ethical opinion exists among us concerning the best way to train children for their place in society. Because of these differences and because of the reluctance to permit a single, iron-cast system of education to be imposed upon a nation compounded of so many strains, we have held that, even though public education is one of our most cherished democratic institutions, the Bill of Rights bars a state from compelling all children to attend the public schools. *Pierce v. Society of Sisters.* But it is a very different thing for this Court to exercise censorship over the conviction of legislatures that a particular program or exercise will best promote in the minds of children who attend the common schools an attachment to the institutions of their country.

What the school authorities are really asserting is the right to awaken in the child's mind considerations as to the significance of the flag contrary to those implanted by the parent. In such an attempt the state is normally at a disadvantage in competing with the parent's authority, so long—and this is the vital aspect of religious toleration—as parents are unmolested in their right to counteract by their own persuasiveness the wisdom and rightness of those loyalties which the state . . . is seeking to promote. Except where the transgression of constitutional liberty is too plain for argument, personal freedom is best maintained—so long as the remedial channels of the democratic process remain open and unobstructed —when it is ingrained in people's habits and not enforced against popular policy by the coercion of adjudicated law. That the flag-salute is an allowable portion of a school program for those who do not invoke conscientious scruples is surely not debatable. But for us to insist that, though the ceremony may be required, exceptional immunity must be given to dissidents, is to maintain that there is no basis for a legislative judgment that such an exemption might introduce elements of difficulty into the school discipline, might cast doubts in the minds of the other children which would themselves weaken the effect of the exercise.

The preciousness of the family relation, the authority and independence which give dignity to parenthood, indeed the enjoyment of all freedom, presuppose the kind of ordered society which is summarized by our flag. A society which is dedicated to the preservation of these ultimate values of civilization may in self-protection utilize the educational process for inculcating those almost unconscious feelings which bind men together in a comprehending loyalty, whatever may be their lesser differences and difficulties. That is to say, the process may be utilized so long as men's right to believe as they please, to win others to their way of belief, and their right to assemble in their chosen places of worship for the devotional ceremonies of their faith, are all fully respected.

The Court's opinion concludes by stating that this is matter for legislative rather than judicial remedy:

Judicial review, itself a limitation on popular government, is a fundamental part of our constitutional scheme. But to the legislature no less than to the courts is committed the guardianship of deeply-cherished liberties. . . . Where all the effective means of inducing political changes are left free from interference, education in the abandonment of foolish legislation is itself a training in liberty. To fight out the wise use of legislative authority in the forum of public opinion and before legislative assemblies rather than to transfer such a contest to the judicial arena, serves to vindicate the self-confidence of a free people.

DISSENTING OPINION OF JUSTICE STONE

Justice Stone's dissenting opinion began by pointing out that in his view there is here a clear violation of the guarantees of free speech and free exercise of religion:

I think the judgment below should be affirmed.

Two youths, now fifteen and sixteen years of age, are by the judgment of this Court held liable to expulsion from the public schools and to denial of all publicly supported educational privileges because of their refusal to yield to the compulsion of a law which commands their participation in a school ceremony contrary to their religious convictions. They and their father are citizens and have not exhibited by any action or statement of opinion, any disloyalty to . . . the United States. They are . . . willing to obey all its laws which do not conflict with what they . . . believe to be the higher commandments of God. It is not doubted that these convictions are religious, that they are genuine, or that the refusal to yield to the compulsion of the law is in good faith . . . It would be a denial of their faith as well as the teachings of most religions to say that children of their age could not have religious convictions.

The law which is thus sustained is unique in the history of Anglo-American legislation. It does more than suppress freedom of speech and more than prohibit free exercise of religion, which concededly are forbidden by the First Amendment and are violations of the liberty guaranteed by the Fourteenth. For by this law the state seeks to coerce these children to express a sentiment which, as they interpret it, they do not entertain, and which violates their . . . religious convictions. It is not denied that such compulsion is a prohibited infringement of personal liberty, freedom of speech and religion, guaranteed by the Bill of Rights, except in so far as it may be justified . . . as a proper exercise of the state's power over public education.

Next, Justice Stone discusses the role of the State's authority over public education and the degree to which this power is subject to constitutional limitations:

Since the state, in competition with parents, may through teaching in the public schools indoctrinate the minds of the young, it is said that in aid of its undertaking to inspire loyalty and devotion to constituted authority and the flag which symbolizes it, may coerce the pupil to make affirmation contrary to his belief and in violation of his religious faith. . . .

Concededly the constitutional guaranties of personal liberty are not always absolutes. Government has a right to survive and powers conferred upon it are not necessarily set at naught by the express prohibitions of the Bill of Rights. It may make war and raise armies. To that end it may compel citizens to give military service, . . . and subject them to military training despite their religious objections. . . . It may suppress religious practices dangerous to morals, and presumably those also which are inimical to public safety, health and good order. . . . But it is a long step, and one which I am unable to take, to the position that government may, as a supposed educational measure and as a means of disciplining the young, compel public affirmations which violate their religious conscience.

The very fact that we have constitutional guaranties of civil liberties and the specificity of their command where freedom of speech and of religion are concerned require some accommodation of the powers which government normally exercises, when no question of civil liberty is involved, to the constitutional demand that those liberties be protected against the action of government itself. The state concededly has power to require and control the education of its citizens, but it cannot by a general law compelling attendance at public schools preclude attendance at a private school adequate in its instruction, where the parent seeks to secure for the child the benefits of religious instruction not provided by the public school. *Pierce v. Society of Sisters.*

The dissenting opinion discusses the nature of civil liberties:

. . . So here, even if we believe that such compulsions will contribute to national unity, there are other ways to teach loyalty and patriotism which are the sources of national unity, than by compelling the pupil to affirm that which he does not believe and by commanding a form of affirmance which violates his religious convictions. Without recourse to such compulsion the state is free to compel attendance at school and require teaching by instruction and study of all in our history and in the structure and organization of our government, including the guaranties of civil liberty which tend to inspire patriotism and love of country. . . .

The guaranties of civil liberty are not guaranties of freedom of the human mind and spirit and of reasonable freedom and opportunity to express them. They presuppose the right of the individual to hold such opinions as he will and to give them reasonably free expression, and his freedom, and that of the state as well, to teach and persuade others by the communication of ideas. The very essence of the liberty which they guaranty is the freedom of the individual from compulsion as to what he shall think and what he shall say, at least where the compulsion is to bear false witness to his religion. If these guaranties are to have any meaning they must, I think, be deemed to withhold from the state any authority to compel belief or the expression of it where that expression violates religious convictions, whatever may be the legislative view of the desirability of such compulsion.

History teaches us that there have been but few infringements of personal liberty by the state which have not been justified, as they are here, in the name of righteousness and the public good, and few which have not been directed, as they are now, at politically helpless minorities. . . . I cannot conceive that in prescribing, as limitations upon the powers of government, the freedom of the mind and spirit secured by the explicit guaranties of freedom of speech and religion, they [the framers] intended or rightly could have left any latitude for a legislative judgment that the compulsory expression of belief which violates religious convictions would better serve the public interest than their protection. The Constitution may well elicit expressions of loyalty to it and to the government which it created, but it does not command such expressions or otherwise give any indication that compulsory expressions of loyalty play any such part in our scheme of government as to override the constitutional protection of freedom of speech and religion. And while such expressions of loyalty, when voluntarily given, may promote national unity, it is quite another matter to say that their compulsory expression by children in violation of their own and their parents' religious convictions can be regarded as playing so important a part in our national unity as to leave school boards free to exact it despite the constitutional guarantee of freedom of religion. The very terms of the Bill of Rights preclude, it seems to me, any reconciliation of such compulsions with the constitutional guaranties by a legislative declaration that they are more important to the public welfare than the Bill of Rights.

The opinion comes to the final conclusion that the Court has an obligation in this case to maintain the right of the plaintiffs to exercise their religious beliefs:

But even if this view be rejected and it is considered that there is some scope for the determination by legislatures whether the citizen shall be compelled to give public expression of such sentiments contrary to his religion, I am not persuaded that we should refrain from passing upon the legislative judgment "as long as the remedial channels of the democratic process remain open and unobstructed." This seems to me no less than the surrender of the constitutional protection of the liberty of small minorities to the popular will. We have previously pointed to the importance of searching judicial inquiry into the legislative judgment in situations where prejudice against discrete and insular minorities may tend to curtail the operation of those political processes ordinarily to be relied on to protect minorities.

. . . And until now we have not hesitated similarly to scrutinize legislation restricting the civil liberty of racial and religious minorities although no political process was affected. *Meyer v. Nebraska, Pierce v. Society of Sisters,* . . . Here we have such a small minority entertaining in good faith a religious belief, which is such a departure from the usual course of human conduct, that most persons are disposed to regard it with little toleration . . . In such circumstances careful scrutiny of legislative efforts to secure conformity of belief and opinion by a compulsory affirmation of the desired belief, is especially needful if civil rights are to receive any protection. Tested by this standard, I am not prepared to say that the right of this small and helpless minority, including children having a strong religious conviction, whether they understand its nature or not, to refrain from an expression obnoxious to their religion, is to be overborne by the interest of the state in maintaining discipline in the schools.

The Constitution expresses more than the conviction of the people that democratic processes must be preserved at all costs. It is also an expression of faith and a command that freedom of mind and spirit must be preserved, which government must obey, if it is to adhere to that justice and moderation without which no free government can exist. For this reason it would seem that legislation which operates to repress the religious freedom of small minorities, which is admittedly within the scope of the protection of the Bill of Rights, must at least be subject to the same judicial scrutiny as legislation which we have recently held to infringe the constitutional liberty of religious and racial minorities.

In brief, the holding in this case was that the Free Exercise Clause of the First Amendment was not violated by the requirement that all school pupils take part in saluting the flag, even including those who claimed to have religious objections to participating.

SOME DOUBTS EXPRESSED

Two years after this decision Justices Black, Douglas, and Murphy who had joined in the majority view in the *Gobitis* case, said in a dissent in the case of *Jones v. Opelika:*

The opinion of the Court sanctions a device which in our opinion suppresses or tends to suppress the free exercise of a religion practiced by a minority group. This is but another step in the direction which *Minersville School District* v. *Gobitis* took against the same religious minority and is a logical extension of the principles upon which that decision rested. Since we joined in the *Gobitis* case we think this is an appropriate occasion to state that we now believe that it also was wrongly decided. Certainly our democratic form of government functioning under the historic Bill of Rights, has a high responsibility to accommodate itself to the religious view of minorities, however unpopular and unorthodox those views may be. The First Amendment does not put the right freely to exercise religion in a subordinate position. We fear, however, that the opinions in these and in the *Gobitis* case do exactly that.

WEST VIRGINIA STATE BOARD OF EDUCATION et al. v. *BARNETTE et al.*[2]

The same question was raised in this case as in the *Gobitis* case. The question was whether a school district could constitutionally require children who claimed religious scruples against taking part in a flag salute to participate in this exercise in the public school classroom.

THE WEST VIRGINIA LAW

Following the *Gobitis* decision, the West Virginia state legislature passed the following law:

In all public, private, parochial and denominational schools located within this state there shall be given regular courses of instruction in history of the United States, in civics, and in the constitutions of the United States and the State of West Virginia, for the purpose of teaching, fostering and perpetuating the ideals, principles and spirit of Americanism, and increasing the knowledge

[2] 319 U.S. 624. Decided June 14, 1943.

of the organization and machinery of the government of the United States and of the state of West Virginia. The state board of education shall, with the advice of the state superintendent of schools, prescribe the courses of study covering these subjects for the public elementary and grammar schools, public high schools and state normal schools.

THE STATE BOARD OF EDUCATION RULING

In January of 1942 the State Board of Education in accordance with that statute adopted a regulation in the preamble of which a great deal of the language from the Supreme Court opinion in the *Gobitis* case was used:

Therefore, be it RESOLVED, that the West Virginia Board of Education does hereby recognize and order that the commonly accepted salute to the Flag of the United States—the right hand is placed upon the breast and the following pledge repeated in unison: "I pledge allegiance to the Flag of the United States of America and to the Republic for which it stands; one Nation, indivisible, with liberty and justice for all"—now becomes a regular part of the program of activities in the public schools, supported in whole or in part by public funds, and that all teachers . . . and pupils in such schools shall be required to participate in the salute, honoring the Nation represented by the Flag; provided, however, that refusal to salute the Flag be regarded as an act of insubordination, and shall be dealt with accordingly.

JEHOVAH'S WITNESSES

The plaintiffs who sought to prevent enforcement of this law and the regulations of the State Board made under the law were members of Jehovah's Witnesses. Of these the Court said:

. . . The Witnesses are an unincorporated body teaching that the obligation imposed by law of God is superior to that of laws enacted by temporal government. Their religious beliefs include a literal version of Exodus, Chapter 20, verses 4 and 5, which says: "Thou shalt not make unto thee any graven image, or any likeness of anything that is in heaven above, or that is in the earth beneath, or that is in the water under the earth; thou shalt not bow down thyself to them nor serve them." They consider that the flag is an "image" within this command. For this reason they refuse to salute it.

The plaintiffs offered to give the following pledge in lieu of the required flag-salute ceremony:

I have pledged my unqualified allegiance and devotion to Jehovah, the Almighty God, and to His Kingdom, for which Jesus commands all Christians to pray.

I respect the flag of the United States and acknowledge it as a symbol of freedom and justice to all.

I pledge allegiance and obedience to all the laws of the United States that are consistent with God's law, as set forth in the Bible.

Chief Justice Hughes and Justice McReynolds had retired since the *Gobitis* decision and Justice Stone was now Chief Justice. Justices Jackson and Rutledge were the new members of the Court.

The three-judge United States District Court which had originally heard the case had, largely on the basis of the wording of the dissent in the *Opelika* case, decided in favor of the plaintiffs. When the case was finally ruled on by the Supreme Court this decision was affirmed by a divided Court. The majority of six was made up of Chief Justice Stone and Justices Black, Douglas, Murphy, Rutledge, and Jackson. The opinion of the Court was written by Justice Jackson and one concurring opinion was filed by Justices Black and Douglas. Another concurring opinion was delivered by Justice Murphy. Justices Roberts and Reed stated that they adhered to the views expressed by the Court in the *Gobitis* case, while an extensive dissenting opinion was written by Justice Frankfurter.

THE OPINION OF THE COURT

Justice Jackson first discussed the features involved in the case:

The freedom asserted by these appellees does not bring them into collision with rights asserted by any other individual. It is such conflicts which most frequently require intervention of the State to determine where the rights of one end and those of another begin. But the refusal of these persons to participate in a ceremony does not interfere or deny rights of others to do so. . . . The sole conflict is between authority and rights of the individual. The State asserts the power to condition access to public education on making a prescribed sign and profession and at the same time to coerce attendance by punishing both parent and child. The latter stand on a right of self-determination in matters that touch individual opinion and personal attitude.

As the present Chief Justice said in dissent in the *Gobitis* case, the State may "require teaching by instruction and study of all in our history and in the structure and organization of our government, including the guaranties of civil liberty, which tend to inspire patriotism and love of country." . . . Here, however, we are dealing with a compulsion of students to declare a belief. They are not merely made acquainted with the flag salute so that they may be informed as to what it is or even what it means. The issue here is whether this slow and easily neglected route to aroused loyalties constitutionally may be short-cut by substituting a compulsory salute and slogan. This issue is not prejudiced by the Court's previous holding that where a State, without compelling attendance, extends college facilities to pupils who voluntarily enroll, it may prescribe military training as part of the course without offense to the Constitution. It was held that those who take advantage of its opportunities may not on ground of conscience refuse compliance with such conditions. . . . In the present case attendance is not optional. That case is also to be distinguished from the present one because, independently of college privileges or requirements, the State has power to raise militia and impose the duties of service therein upon its citizens.

There is no doubt that, in connection with the pledges, the flag salute is a form of utterance. Symbolism is a primitive but effective way of communicating ideas. The use of an emblem or flag to symbolize some system, idea, institution, or personality, is a short cut from mind to mind. Causes and nations, political parties, lodges and ecclesiastical groups seek to knit the loyalty of their followings to a flag or banner, a color or design. The State announces rank, function, and authority through crowns and maces, uniforms and black robes; the Church speaks through the Cross, the Crucifix, the altar and shrine, and clerical raiment. Symbols of State often convey political ideas just as religious symbols come to convey theological ones. Associated with many of these symbols are appropriate gestures of acceptance or respect; a salute, a bowed or bared head, a bended knee. A person gets from a symbol the meaning he puts into it, and what is one man's comfort and inspiration is another's jest and scorn.

A footnote at this point is of interest:

Early Christians were frequently persecuted for their refusal to participate in ceremonies before the statue of the emperor or other symbol of imperial authority. The story of William Tell's sentence to shoot an apple off his son's head for refusal to salute a bailiff's hat is an ancient one. . . . The Quakers, William Penn included, suffered punishment rather than uncover their heads in deference to any civil authority. . . .

The nature of the issue raised is further analyzed:

It is also to be noted that the compulsory flag salute and pledge requires affirmation of a belief and an attitude of mind. It is not clear whether the regulation contemplates that pupils forego any contrary convictions of their own and become unwilling converts to the prescribed ceremony or whether it will be acceptable if they simulate assent by words without belief and by a gesture barren of meaning. It is now a commonplace that censorship or suppression of expression of opinion is tolerated by our Constitution only when the expression presents a clear and present danger of action of a kind the State is empowered to prevent and punish. It would seem that involuntary affirmation could be commanded only on even more immediate and urgent grounds than silence. But here the power of compulsion is invoked without any allegation that remaining passive during a flag salute ritual creates a clear and present danger that would justify an effort even to muffle expression. To sustain the compulsory flag salute we are required to say that a Bill of Rights which guards the individual's right to speak his own mind, left it open to public authorities to compel him to utter what is not in his mind.

Whether the First Amendment to the Constitution will permit officials to order observance of a ritual of this nature does not depend upon whether as a voluntary exercise we would think it to be good, bad or merely innocuous. . . . Hence validity of the asserted power to force an American citizen publicly to profess any statement of belief or to engage in any ceremony of assent to one, presents questions of power that must be considered independently of any idea we may have as to the utility of the ceremony in question.

Nor does the issue as we see it turn on one's possession of particular religious views or the sincerity with which they are held. While religion supplies appellee's motive for enduring the discomforts of making the issue in this case, many citizens who do not share these religious views hold such a compulsory rite to infringe constitutional liberty of the individual. It is not necessary to inquire whether nonconformist beliefs will exempt from the duty to salute unless we first find power to make the salute a legal duty.

The opinion then considers the arguments offered in the *Gobitis* decision:

. . . we reexamine against this broader definition of issues in this case, specific grounds assigned for the *Gobitis* decision:
1. It was said that the flag-salute controversy confronted the Court with the problem which Lincoln cast in memorable dilemma: "Must a government of necessity be too *strong* for the liberties of its people, or too *weak* to maintain its own existence?" and that the answer must be in favor of strength.
We think these issues may be examined free of pressure or restraint growing out of such considerations.

It may be doubted whether Mr. Lincoln would have thought that the strength of government to maintain itself would be impressively vindicated by our confirming power of the State to expel a handful of children from school. Such oversimplification, so handy in political debate, often lacks the precision necessary to postulates of judicial reasoning.

Government of limited power need not be anemic government. Assurance that rights are secure tends to diminish fear and jealousy of strong government, and by making us feel safe to live under it, makes for its better support. Without promise of a limiting Bill of Rights it is doubtful if our Constitution could have mustered enough strength to enable its ratification. To enforce those rights today is not to choose weak government over strong government. It is only to adhere as a means of strength to individual freedom of mind in preference to officially disciplined uniformity for which history indicates a disappointing and disastrous end.

The subject now before us exemplifies this principle. Free public education, if faithful to the ideal of secular instruction and political neutrality, will not be partisan or enemy of any class, creed, party, or faction. If it is to impose any ideological discipline, however, each party or denomination must seek to control, or failing that, to weaken the influence of the educational system. Observance of the limitations of the Constitution will not weaken government in the field appropriate for its exercise.

2. It was also considered in the *Gobitis* case that functions of educational officers in States, counties and school districts were such that to interfere with their authority "would in effect make us the school board for the country."

The Fourteenth Amendment, as now applied to the States, protects the citizen against the State itself and all of its creatures— Boards of Education not excepted. These have, of course, important, delicate, and highly discretionary functions, but none that they may not perform within the limits of the Bill of Rights. That they are educating the young for citizenship is reason for scrupulous protection of Constitutional freedoms of the individual, if we are not to strangle the free mind at its source and teach youth to discount important principles of our government as mere platitudes.

3. The *Gobitis* opinion reasoned that this is a field "where

courts possess no marked and certainly no controlling competence," that it is committed to the legislatures as well as the courts to guard cherished liberties and that it is constitutionally appropriate to "fight out the wise use of legislative authority in the forum of public opinion and before legislative assemblies rather than to transfer such a contest to the judicial arena," since all the effective means of inducing political changes are left free.

The very purpose of a Bill of Rights was to withdraw certain subjects from the vicissitudes of political controversy, to place them beyond the reach of majorities and officials and to establish them as legal principles to be applied by the courts. One's right to life, liberty, and property, to free speech, a free press, freedom of worship and assembly, and other fundamental rights may not be submitted to vote; they depend on the outcome of no elections.

In weighing the arguments of the parties it is important to distinguish between the due process clause of the Fourteenth Amendment as an instrument for transmitting the principles of the First Amendment and those cases in which it is applied for its own sake. The test of legislation which collides with the Fourteenth Amendment, because it also collides with the principles of the First, is much more definite than the test when only the Fourteenth is involved. Much of the vagueness of the due process clause disappears when the specific prohibitions of the First become its standard. . . . freedoms of speech and of press, of assembly, and of worship may not be infringed on . . . slender grounds. They are susceptible of restriction only to prevent grave and immediate danger to interests which the State may lawfully protect. It is important to note that while it is the Fourteenth Amendment which bears directly upon the State it is the more specific limiting principles of the First Amendment that finally govern this case.

Nor does our duty to apply the Bill of Rights to assertions of official authority depend upon our possession of marked competence in the field where the invasion of rights occurs. True, the task of translating the majestic generalities of the Bill of Rights, conceived as part of the pattern of liberal government in the eighteenth century, into concrete restraints on officials dealing with the problems of the twentieth century, is one to disturb self-confidence. These principles grew in soil which also produced a philosophy that the individual was the center of society, that his liberty was attainable through mere absence of governmental restraints, and that government should be entrusted with few controls and only the mildest supervision over men's affairs. . . . But we act in these matters not by authority of our competence but by force of our commissions. We cannot, because of modest estimates of our competence in such specialties as public education, withhold the judgment that history authenticates as the function of this Court when liberty is infringed.

4. Lastly, and this is the very heart of the *Gobitis* opinion, it reasons that "National unity is the basis of national security," that the authorities have "the right to select appropriate means for its attainment," and hence reaches the conclusion that such compulsory measures toward "national unity" are constitutional. Upon the verity of this assumption depends our answer in this case.

National unity as an end which officials may foster by persuasion and example is not in question. The problem is whether under our Constitution compulsion as here employed is a permissible means for its achievement.

Struggles to coerce uniformity of sentiment in support of some end thought essential to their time and country have been waged by many good as well as by evil men. Nationalism is a relatively recent phenomenon but at other times and places the ends have been racial or territorial security, support of a dynasty or regime, and particular plans for saving souls. As first and moderate methods to attain unity have failed, those bent on its accomplishment must resort to an ever-increasing severity. As governmental pressure toward unity becomes greater, so strife becomes more bitter as to whose unity it shall be. Probably no deeper division of our people could proceed from any provocation than from finding it necessary to choose what doctrine and whose program public educational officials shall compel youth to unite in embracing. Ultimate futility of such attempts to compel coherence is the lesson of every such effort from the Roman drive to stamp out Christianity as a disturber of its pagan unity, the Inquisition, as a means to religious and dynastic unity, the Siberian exiles as a means to Russian unity, down to the fast failing efforts of our present totalitarian enemies. Those who begin coercive elimination of dissent soon find themselves exterminating dissenters. . . .

It seems trite but necessary to say that the First Amendment to our Constitution was designed to avoid these ends by avoiding these beginnings. . . . We set up government by consent of the governed, and the Bill of Rights denies those in power any legal opportunity to coerce that consent. Authority here is to be controlled by public opinion, not public opinion by authority.

. The case is made difficult not because the principles of its decision are obscure but because the flag involved is our own. Nevertheless, we apply the limitations of the Constitution with no fear that freedom to be intellectually and spiritually diverse or even contrary will disintegrate the social organization. To believe that patriotism will not flourish if patriotic ceremonies are voluntary and spontaneous instead of a compulsory routine is to make an unflattering estimate of the appeal of our institutions to free minds. We can have intellectual individualism and the rich cultural diversities that we owe to exceptional minds only at the price of occasional eccentricity and abnormal attitudes. When they are so harmless to others or to the State as those we deal with here, the price is not too great. But freedom to differ is not limited to things that do not matter much. That would be a mere shadow of freedom. The test of its substance is the right to differ as to things that touch the heart of the existing order.

If there is any fixed star in our constitutional constellation, it is that no official, high or petty, can prescribe what shall be orthodox in politics, nationalism, religion or other matters of opinion or force citizens to confess by word or act their faith therein. If there are any circumstances which permit an exception, they do not now occur to us.

We think the action of the local authorities in compelling the flag salute and pledge transcends constitutional limitations on their power and invades the sphere of intellect and spirit which it is the purpose of the First Amendment to our Constitution to reserve from all official control.

In its concluding paragraph the Court's decision specifically overrules the ruling in the *Gobitis* case:

The decision of this Court in *Minersville School District* v. *Gobitis* and the holdings of those few *per curiam* decisions which preceded and foreshadowed it are overruled . . .

A CONCURRING OPINION

Justices Black and Douglas stated their views as follows:

We are substantially in agreement with the opinion just read, but since we originally joined with the Court in the *Gobitis* case, it is appropriate that we make a brief statement of reasons for our change of view.

Reluctance to make the Federal Constitution a rigid bar against state regulation of conduct thought inimical to the public welfare was the controlling influence which moved us to consent to the *Gobitis* decision. Long reflection convinced us that although the principle is sound, its application in the particular case was wrong. We believe that the statute before us fails to accord full scope to the freedom of religion secured to the appellees by the First and Fourteenth Amendments.

The statute requires the appellees to participate in a ceremony aimed at inculcating respect for the flag and for this country. The Jehovah's Witnesses, without any desire to show disrespect for either the flag or the country, interpret the Bible as commanding, at the risk of God's displeasure, that they not go through the form of a pledge of allegiance to any flag. The devoutness of their belief is evidenced by their willingness to suffer persecution and punishment rather than make the pledge. No well-ordered society can leave to the individuals an absolute right to make final decisions, unassailable by the State, as to everything they will or will not do. The First Amendment does not go so far. Religious faiths, honestly held, do not free individuals from responsibility to conduct themselves obediently to laws which are either imperatively necessary to protect society as a whole from grave and pressingly imminent dangers or which, without any general prohibition, merely regulate time, place, or manner of religious activity. Decision as to the constitutionality of particular laws which strike at the substance of religious tenets and practices must be made by this Court. The duty is a solemn one, and in meeting it we cannot say that a failure, because of religious scruples, to assume a particular physical position and to repeat the words of a patriotic formula creates a grave danger to the nation. . . .

Words uttered under coercion are proof of loyalty to nothing but self-interest. Love of country must spring from willing hearts and free minds, . . .

Neither our domestic tranquility in peace nor our martial effort in war depend on compelling little children to participate in a ceremony which ends in nothing for them but a fear of spiritual condemnation. If, as we think, their fears are groundless, time and reason are the proper antidotes for their errors. The ceremonial, when enforced against conscientious objectors, more likely to defeat than to serve its high purpose, is a handy implement for disguised religious persecution. As such, it is inconsistent with our Constitution's plan and purpose.

CONCURRING OPINION BY JUSTICE MURPHY

Justice Murphy in his opinion said in part:

A reluctance to interfere with considered state action, the fact that the end sought is a desirable one, the emotion aroused by the flag as a symbol for which we have fought and are now fighting again—all of these are understandable. But there is before us the right of freedom to believe, freedom to worship one's Maker according to the dictates of one's conscience, a right which the Constitution specifically shelters. Reflection has convinced me that as a judge I have no loftier duty or responsibility than to uphold that spiritual freedom to its farthest reaches.

The right of freedom of thought and of religion as guaranteed by the Constitution against State action includes both the right to speak freely and the right to refrain from speaking at all, except insofar as essential operations of government may require it for the preservation of an orderly society, as in the case of compulsion to give evidence in court. . . . To many it is deeply distasteful to join in a public chorus of affirmation of private belief. By some, including the members of this sect, it is apparently regarded as incompatible with a primary religious obligation and therefore a restriction on religious freedom. Official compulsion to affirm what is contrary to one's religious beliefs is the antithesis of freedom of worship which, it is well to recall, was achieved in this country only after what Jefferson characterized as the "severest contests in which I have ever been engaged."

I am unable to agree that the benefits that may accrue to society from the compulsory flag salute are sufficiently definite and tangible to justify the invasion of freedom and privacy that is entailed . . . The trenchant words in the preamble to the Virginia Statute for Religious Freedom remain unanswerable: ". . . all attempts to influence the mind by temporal punishments, or burdens, or by civil incapacitations, tend only to beget habits of hypocrisy and meanness, . . ." Any spark of love for country which may be generated in a child or his associates by forcing him to make what is to him an empty gesture and recite words wrung from him contrary to his religious beliefs is overshadowed by the desirability of preserving freedom of conscience to the full. . . .

DISSENTING OPINION

Justice Frankfurter in the first part of his dissent described the dilemma facing him:

One who belongs to the most vilified and persecuted minority in history is not likely to be insensible to the freedoms guaranteed by our Constitution. Were my purely personal attitude relevant I should wholeheartedly associate myself with the general libertarian views in the Court's opinion, representing as they do the thought and action of a lifetime. But as judges we are neither Jew nor Gentile, neither Catholic nor agnostic. We owe equal attachment to the Constitution and are equally bound by our judicial obligations whether we derive our citizenship from the earliest or the latest immigrants to these shores. As a member of this Court I am not justified in writing my private notions of policy into the Constitution, no matter how deeply I may cherish them or how mischievous I may deem their disregard. The duty of a judge who must decide which of two claims before the Court shall prevail, that of a State to enact and enforce laws within its general competence or that of an individual to refuse obedience because of the demands of his conscience, is not that of the ordinary person. It can never be emphasized too much that one's own opinion about the wisdom or evil of a law should be excluded altogether when one is doing one's duty on the bench. The only opinion of our own even looking in that direction that is material is our opinion whether legislators could in reason have enacted such a law. In the light of all the circumstances, including the history of this question in this Court, it would require more daring than I possess to deny that reasonable legislators could have taken the action which is before us for review. Most unwillingly, therefore, I must differ from my brethren with regard to legislation like this. I cannot bring my mind to believe that the "liberty" secured by the Due Process Clause gives this Court authority to deny to the State of West Virginia the attainment of that which we all recognize as a legitimate legislative end, namely, the promotion of good citizenship, by employment of the means here chosen.

After a lengthy discussion of the Court's proper role in declaring legislative enactments void, Justice Frankfurter discusses his concept of the meaning of the freedom of religion guaranties in the First Amendment:

What one can say with assurance is that the history out of which grew constitutional provisions for religious equality and the writings of the great exponents of religious freedom—Jefferson, Madison, John Adams, Benjamin Franklin—are totally wanting in justification for a claim by dissidents of exceptional immunity from civic measures of general applicability, measures not in fact disguised assaults upon such dissident views. The great leaders of the American Revolution were determined to remove political support from every religious establishment. They put on an equality the different religious sects . . . which, as dissenters, had been under the heel of the various orthodoxies that prevailed in different colonies. So far as the state was concerned there was to be neither orthodoxy nor heterodoxy. And so Jefferson and those who followed him wrote guaranties of religious freedom into our constitutions. Religious minorities as well as religious majorities were to be equal in the eyes of the political state. But Jefferson and the others also knew that minorities may disrupt society. It never would have occurred to them to write into the Constitution the subordination of the general civil authority of the state to sectarian scruples.

The constitutional protection of religious freedom terminated disabilities, it did not create new privileges. It gave religious equality, not civil immunity. Its essence is freedom from conformity to religious dogma, not freedom from conformity to law because of religious dogma. . . . Otherwise each individual could set up his own censor against obedience to laws conscientiously deemed for the public good by those whose business it is to make laws.

The essence of the religious freedom guaranteed by our Constitution is therefore this: no religion shall either receive the state's support or incur its hostility. Religion is outside the sphere of political government. This does not mean that all matters on which religious organizations or beliefs may pronounce are outside the sphere of government. Were this so, instead of the separation of church and state, there would be the subordination of the state on any matter deemed within the sovereignty of the religious conscience. Much that is the concern of temporal authority affects the spiritual interests of men. But is not enough to strike down a nondiscriminatory law that it may hurt or offend some dissident view. It would be too easy to cite numerous prohibitions and injunctions to which laws run counter if the variant interpretations of the Bible were made the tests of obedience to law. The validity of secular laws cannot be measured by their conformity to religious doctrines. It is only in a theocratic state that ecclesiastical doctrines measure legal right or wrong.

An act compelling profession of allegiance to a religion, no matter how subtly or tenuously promoted, is bad. But an act promoting good citizenship and national allegiance is within the domain of governmental authority and is therefore to be judged by the same considerations of power and of constitutionality as those involved in the many claims of immunity from civil obedience because of religious scruples.

That claims are pressed on behalf of sincere religious convictions does not of itself establish their constitutional validity.

Law is concerned with external behavior and not with the inner life of man. Socrates lives in history partly because he gave his life for the conviction that duty of obedience to secular law does not presuppose consent to its enactment or belief in its virtue. The consent upon which free government rests is the consent that comes from sharing in the process of making and unmaking laws. The state is not shut out from a domain because the individual conscience may deny the state's claim. The individual conscience may profess what faith it chooses. It may affirm and promote that faith —in the language of the Constitution, it may "exercise" it freely— but it cannot thereby restrict community action through political organs in matters of community concern, so long as the action is not asserted in a discriminatory way either openly or by stealth. One may have the right to practice one's religion and at the same time owe the duty of formal obedience to laws that run counter to one's beliefs. Compelling belief implies denial of opportunity to combat it and to assert dissident views. Such compulsion is one thing. Quite another matter is the submission to conformity of action while denying its wisdom or virtue and with ample opportunity for seeking its change or abrogation.

In *Hamilton v. Regents*, this Court unanimously held that one attending a state-maintained university cannot refuse attendance on courses that offend his religious scruples. That decision is not overruled today, but is distinguished on the ground that attendance at the institution for higher education was voluntary and therefore a student could not refuse compliance with its conditions and yet take advantage of its opportunities. But West Virginia does not compel the attendance at its public schools of the children here concerned. West Virginia does not so compel, for it cannot. This Court denied the right of a state to require its children to attend public schools. *Pierce v. Society of Sisters*. As to its public schools, West Virginia imposes conditions which it deems necessary in the development of future citizens precisely as California deemed necessary the requirements that offended the student's conscience in the *Hamilton* case. . . . I find it impossible, so far as constitutional power is concerned, to differentiate what was sanctioned in the *Hamilton* case from what is nullified in this case. And for me it still remains to be explained why the grounds of Mr. Justice Cardozo's opinion in *Hamilton v. Regents*, are not sufficient to sustain the flag salute requirement. Such a requirement, like the requirement in the *Hamilton* case, "is not an interference by the state with the free exercise of religion when the liberties of the constitution are read in the light of a century and a half of history during days of peace and war." The religious worshipper "if his liberties were to be thus extended, might refuse to contribute taxes . . . in furtherance of any other end condemned by his conscience as irreligious or immoral. The right of private judgment has never yet been so exalted above the powers and the compulsion of the agencies of government."

The nature of the obligation assumed when a child is enrolled in a public school is examined:

/ Parents have the privilege of choosing which schools they wish their children to attend. And the question here is whether the state may make certain requirements that seem to it to be desirable or important for the proper education of those future citizens who go to the schools maintained by the states, or whether the pupils in those schools may be relieved from those requirements if they run counter to the consciences of their parents. Not only have parents the right to send children to schools of their own choosing but the state has no right to bring such schools "under a strict governmental control" or give "affirmative direction concerning the intimate and essential details of such schools, entrust their control to public officers, and deny both owners and patrons reasonable choice and discretion in respect to teachers, curriculum, and textbooks." . . . Why should not the state likewise have constitutional power to make reasonable provisions for the proper instruction of children in schools maintained by it?

Consider the controversial issue of compulsory Bible-reading in public schools. The educational policies of the states are in great conflict over this, and the state courts are divided in their decisions on the issue whether the requirement of Bible-reading offends constitutional provisions dealing with religious freedom. The requirement of Bible-reading has been justified by various state courts as an appropriate means of inculcating ethical precepts and familiarizing pupils with the most lasting expression of great English literature. Is this Court to overthrow such variant educational policies by denying states the right to entertain such convictions in regard to their school systems, because of a belief that the King James version is in fact a sectarian text to which parents of the Catholic and Jewish faiths and of some Protestant persuasions may rightly object to having their children exposed? On the other hand the religious consciences of some parents may rebel at the absence of any Bible-reading in the schools. . . . The religious consciences of some parents may be offended by subjecting their children to the Biblical account of creation, while another state may offend parents by prohibiting a teaching of biology that contradicts such Biblical account.

There are other issues in the offing which admonish us of the difficulties and complexities that confront states in the duty of administering their local school systems. All citizens are taxed for the support of public schools although this Court has denied the right of a state to compel all children to go to such schools and has recognized the right of parents to send children to privately maintained schools. Parents who are dissatisfied with the public schools thus carry a double educational burden. Children who go to public school enjoy in many states derivative advantages such as free textbooks, free lunch, and free transportation in going to and from school. What of the claims for equality of treatment of those parents who, because of religious scruples, cannot send their children to public schools? What of the claim that if the right to send children to privately maintained schools is partly an exercise of religious conviction, to render effective this right it should be accompanied by equality of treatment by the state in supplying free textbooks, free lunch, and free transportation to children who go to private schools? What of the claim that such grants are offensive to the cardinal constitutional doctrine of separation of church and state?

We are told that a flag salute is a doubtful substitute for adequate understanding of our institutions. The states that require such a school exercise do not have to justify it as the only means for promoting good citizenship in children, but merely as one of diverse means for accomplishing a worthy end. We may deem it a foolish measure, but the point is that this Court is not the organ of government to resolve doubts as to whether it will fulfill its purpose. Only if there be no doubt that any reasonable mind could entertain can we deny to the states the right to resolve doubts their way and not ours.

That which to the majority may seem essential for the welfare of the state may offend the conscience of a minority. But, so long as no inroads are made upon the actual exercise of religion by the minority, to deny the political power of the majority to enact laws concerned with civil matters, simply because they may offend the consciences of a minority, really means that the consciences of a minority are more sacred and more enshrined in the Constitution than the consciences of the majority.

We are told that symbolism is a dramatic but primitive way of communicating ideas. Symbolism is inescapable. Even the most sophisticated live by symbols. But it is not for this Court to make psychological judgments as to the effectiveness of a particular symbol in inculcating concededly indispensable feelings, particularly if the state happens to see fit to utilize the symbol that represents our heritage and our hopes. . . .

The right of West Virginia to utilize the flag salute as part of its educational process is denied because, so it is argued, it cannot be justified as a means of meeting a "clear and present danger" to national unity. In passing it deserves to be noted that the four cases which unanimously sustained the power of states to utilize such an educational measure arose and were all decided before the present World War. But to measure the state's power to make such regulations as are here resisted by the imminence of national danger is wholly to misconceive the origin and purpose of the concept of "clear and present danger." To apply such a test is for the Court to assume, however unwittingly, a legislative responsibility that does not belong to it. To talk about "clear and present danger" as the touchstone of allowable educational policy by the states whatever school curricula may impinge upon the boundaries of individual conscience, is to take a felicitous phrase out of the context of the particular situation where it arose and for which it was adapted. Mr. Justice Holmes used the phrase "clear and present danger" in a case involving mere speech as a means by which alone to accomplish sedition in time of war. By that phrase he meant merely to indicate that, in view of the protection given to utterance by the

First Amendment, in order that mere utterance may not be proscribed, "the words used are used in such circumstances and are of such a nature as to create a clear and present danger that they will bring about the substantive evils that Congress has a right to prevent." . . . The "substantive evils" about which he was speaking were inducement of insubordination in the military and naval forces of the United States and obstruction of enlistment while the country was at war. He was not enunciating a formal rule that there can be no restriction upon speech and, still less, no compulsion where conscience balks, unless imminent danger would thereby be wrought "to our institutions or our government."

After returning to a further searching examination of the proper role of courts in striking down legislation on the ground of unconstitutionality, the dissenting opinion by Justice Frankfurter concludes:

Of course patriotism can not be enforced by the flag salute. But neither can the liberal spirit be enforced by judicial invalidation of illiberal legislation. Our constant preoccupation with the constitutionality of legislation rather than with its wisdom tends to preoccupation of the American mind with a false value. The tendency of focusing attention on constitutionality is to make constitutionality synonymous with wisdom, to regard a law as all right if it is constitutional. Such an attitude is a great enemy of liberalism. Particularly in legislation affecting freedom of thought and freedom of speech much which should offend a free-spirited society is constitutional. Reliance for the most precious interests of civilization, therefore, must be found outside of their vindication in courts of law. Only a persistent positive translation of the faith of a free society into the convictions and habits and actions of a community is the ultimate reliance against unabated temptations to fetter the human spirit.

The ruling in this case was that under the Free Exercise Clause of the First Amendment a school district could not legally require all pupils in public schools to take part in the flag salute when some objected on the grounds of religious scruples. This was an explicit reversal of the *Gobitis* decision.

SUMMARY

1. In *Minersville* v. *Gobitis* a school regulation requiring all public school pupils to salute the flag was challenged by members of Jehovah's Witnesses on the ground that their religious beliefs would not allow them to take part in such a ceremony.

2. The Supreme Court decided that the regulation was a valid one and well within legislative power and discretion. The Court, in an opinion written by Justice Frankfurter, stated that the religious rights of the children under the First Amendment were not infringed.

3. In a dissenting opinion, Justice Stone stated that in his view the rights of the children under the Free Exercise Clause of the First Amendment were infringed and that legislative judgments such as this were subject to judicial review.

4. Two years later in *Jones* v. *Opelika*, Justices Black, Douglas, and Murphy, who had joined in the majority decision in the *Gobitis* case, expressed doubts as to the correctness of that decision.

5. In *West Virginia* v. *Barnette* (1943) the identical question previously posed was once again brought to the Supreme Court.

6. The Supreme Court in a 6–3 decision specifically overruled its previous decision and held that the requirement that all pupils participate in saluting the flag was an infringement of the constitutional rights of those children whose religious beliefs were such as to make participation objectionable to them.

7. Justice Frankfurter vigorously dissented. He pointed out that regardless of his personal views as to the wisdom of the regulation in question, the matter was one for legislative determination.

8. The holding in the *Hamilton* case to the effect that a student at a land-grant college could not insist on being excused from ROTC training because of religious scruples was distinguished from the *Barnette* ruling by the majority of the Court on the ground that in *Hamilton* there was no compulsory attendance requirement.

CHAPTER 5

THE "CHILD BENEFIT
THEORY"

Two cases have been decided by the United States Supreme Court which involved the expenditure of tax money for purposes related to pupils attending nonpublic schools sponsored by religious organizations.

In the *Cochran* case, a Louisiana statute providing for the supplying of secular textbooks was under attack. In this case, decided in 1930, the decision did not turn on the First Amendment. The *Everson* case, decided 17 years later, is the classic case dealing with the First Amendment's Establishment of Religion clause. Here the validity of a New Jersey statute allowing school districts to pay the cost of pupils' transportation to and from parochial schools was involved.

COCHRAN et al. v. LOUISIANA STATE
BOARD OF EDUCATION et al.[1]

THE LOUISIANA STATUTE

At issue in this case was the validity of a Louisiana statute which provided for the use of tax money for "supplying school

[1] 281 U.S. 370. Decided April 28, 1930.

books to the school children of the State." It was contended by the plaintiff that using a portion of these tax moneys for the purchase of secular textbooks to be furnished to children attending other than public schools was a violation of the Fourteenth Amendment. It is interesting to note that the argument and decision in this case turned on the provision of that Amendment forbidding the taking of private property for private use. The First Amendment was not mentioned at all.

The Supreme Court disposed of this case in a very short opinion which consisted largely of the quotation of a passage from the opinion of the Louisiana Supreme Court which had upheld the validity of the procedure complained of.

OPINION OF THE SUPREME COURT

The Court said:

The contention of the appellant under the Fourteenth Amendment is that taxation for the purpose of school books constituted a taking of private property for a private purpose. . . . The purpose is said to be to aid private, religious, sectarian, and other schools not embraced in the public educational system of the State by furnishing textbooks free to the children attending such private schools. The operation and effect of the legislation in question were described by the Supreme Court of the State as follows:

One may scan the acts in vain to ascertain where any money is appropriated for the purchase of school books for the use of any church, private, sectarian or even public school. The appropriations were made for the specific purpose of purchasing school books for the use of the school children of the state, free of cost to them. It was for their benefit and the resulting benefit to the state that the appropriations were made. True, these children attend some school, public or private, the latter, sectarian or non-sectarian, and that the books are to be furnished them for their use, free of cost, whichever they attend. The schools, however, are not the beneficiaries of these appropriations. They obtain nothing from them, nor are they relieved of a single obligation, because of them. The school children and the state alone are the beneficiaries. . . . What the statutes contemplate is that the same books that are furnished children attending public schools shall be furnished children attending private schools. . . . Among these books naturally, none is to be expected, adapted to religious instruction.

Viewing the statute as having the effect thus attributed to it, we can not doubt that the taxing power of the State is exerted for a public purpose. The legislation does not segregate private schools, or their pupils, as its beneficiaries or attempt to interfere with any matters of exclusively private concern. Its interest is education, broadly; its method comprehensive. . . .

The Court ruled in this case that there was no constitutional objection to a state providing secular textbooks to nonpublic school pupils. It was held that this act was for the children's benefit and not a form of state aid to nonpublic schools.

EVERSON v. BOARD OF EDUCATION OF THE TOWNSHIP OF EWING et al.[2]

THE NEW JERSEY LAW

A New Jersey statute reads as follows:

Whenever in any district there are children living remote from any schoolhouse, the board of education of the district may make rules and contracts for the transportation of such children to and from school, including the transportation of school children to and from school other than a public school, except such school as is operated for profit. . . .

THE SCHOOL BOARD REGULATION

Ewing Township, located near the City of Trenton, did not maintain a high school. Accordingly, high school pupils travelled by public transportation to neighboring school districts. In order to provide for the semiannual reimbursement of the expense of this transportation to parents, the school board passed the following resolution:

[2] 330 U.S. 1. Decided February 10, 1947.

The transportation committee recommended the transportation of pupils of Ewing to the Trenton and Pennington High Schools and Catholic Schools by way of public carrier. . . . the same was adopted.

The plaintiff, as a taxpayer, brought suit to have the practice of reimbursing parents of children attending Catholic parochial schools declared invalid under the provisions of the First Amendment (made applicable to the states by the Fourteenth). Other grounds were also urged by the plaintiff but will not be discussed in this chapter.

DECISION OF THE NEW JERSEY LOWER COURT

The case was first decided by the Supreme Court of New Jersey in September, 1944. The holding by a vote of two to one was that such payments were unconstitutional as an aid to religious schools. The majority pointed out that the conflict between the decisions rendered in varying states had never been resolved but adopted the view that such payments were in effect a state disbursement of tax moneys for the benefit of a religious institution in violation of constitutional provisions. The dissenting judge, however, stated:

Such transportation is a service to the children and their parents rather than to the schools. . . . It is in no real sense a contribution to "the use" or the maintenance of the institutions which the children attend.

DECISION OF THE NEW JERSEY HIGHER COURT

In October, 1945, this decision was reversed by the Court of Errors and Appeals of New Jersey. The court (6–3) rather summarily disposed of the arguments advanced by the plaintiff saying that this provision for payment was in support of and supplementary to the school attendance laws of New Jersey.

The dissenting judges rejected the theory that these payments were for the benefit of the child rather than for the benefit of the religious school. The dissenting opinion uses the following language:

Among its (the so-called child benefit theory) weaknesses as a means of avoiding constitutional inhibitions are its vagueness and the impossibility of satisfactorily distinguishing one item of expense from another in the long process of child education. . . . There is no logical stopping point. . . . Every step in the educational process is, presumably, for the benefit of the child and, therefore, theoretically for the benefit of the state. Consequently, if the argument is sound, it is within the discretion of the legislature, free of constitutional restraint, to provide for practically the entire cost of education in private and parochial schools as well as in public schools.

The plaintiff then appealed to the United States Supreme Court which decided the case in February, 1947. As we shall see from the following, the Court was sharply divided. The majority was made up of Chief Justice Vinson, Justice Black, who wrote the opinion, and Justices Reed, Douglas, and Murphy. (It is an interesting sidelight that Justice Douglas in 1962 in his concurring opinion in the *Engel* case [see Chapter 7] said "The *Everson* case seems in retrospect to be out of line with the First Amendment.") The minority was composed of Justices Frankfurter, Jackson, Rutledge, and Burton. A dissenting opinion written by Justice Jackson was concurred in by Justice Frankfurter and all four dissenting Justices joined in the lengthy and exhaustive opinion written by Justice Rutledge.

THE OPINION OF THE SUPREME COURT

Justice Black's opinion opened with a statement of the facts and issues involved:

A New Jersey statute authorizes its local school districts to make rules and contracts for the transportation of children to and from schools. The appellee, a township board of education, acting pursuant to this statute, authorized reimbursement to parents of money expended by them for the bus transportation of their children on regular busses operated by the public transportation system. Part of this money was for the payment of transportation of some children in the community to Catholic parochial schools. These church schools give their students, in addition to secular education, regular religious instruction. . . .

The appellant, in his capacity as a district taxpayer, filed suit in a state court challenging the right of the Board to reimburse parents of parochial school students.

The only contention here is that the state statute and the resolution, insofar as they authorized reimbursement to parents of children attending parochial schools, violate the Federal Constitution in these two respects, which to some extent overlap. *First.* They authorize the State to take by taxation the private property of some and bestow it upon others, to be used for their own private purposes. This, it is alleged, violates the due process clause of the Fourteenth Amendment. *Second.* The statute and the resolution forced inhabitants to pay taxes to help support and maintain schools which are dedicated to, and which regularly teach, the Catholic Faith. This is alleged to be a use of state power to support church schools contrary to the prohibition of the First Amendment. . . .

Justice Black then turns to the contention that the New Jersey practice was in violation of the Establishment Clause of the First Amendment. He first reviews some of the history and political philosophy underlying its adoption.

Second. The New Jersey statute is challenged as a "law respecting an establishment of religion." The First Amendment as made applicable to the states by the Fourteenth . . . commands that a state "shall make no law respecting an establishment of religion, or prohibiting the free exercise thereof. . . ." Once again, therefore, it is not inappropriate briefly to review the background and environment of the period in which that constitutional language was fashioned and adopted.

A large proportion of the early settlers of this country came here from Europe to escape the bondage of laws which compelled them to support and attend government-favored churches. The centuries immediately before and contemporaneous with the colonization of America had been filled with turmoil, civil strife, and persecutions, generated in large part by established sects determined to maintain their absolute political and religious supremacy. With the power of government supporting them, at various times and places, Catholics had persecuted Protestants, Protestants had persecuted Catholics, Protestant sects had persecuted other Protestant sects, Catholics of one shade of belief had persecuted Catholics of another shade of belief, and all of these had from time to time persecuted Jews. In efforts to force loyalty to whatever religious group happened to be on top and in league with the government of a particular time and place, men and women had been fined, cast in jail, cruelly tortured, and killed. Among the offenses for which these punishments had been inflicted were such things as speaking disrespectfully of the views of ministers of government established churches, non-attendance at those churches, expressions of non-belief in their doctrines, and failure to pay taxes and tithes to support them.

These practices of the old world were transplanted to and began to thrive in the soil of the new America. . . . These practices became so commonplace as to shock the freedom-loving colonials into a feeling of abhorrence. The imposition of taxes to pay ministers' salaries and to build and maintain churches and church property aroused their indignation. It was these feelings which found expression in the First Amendment.

The meaning and scope of the First Amendment, preventing establishment of religion or prohibiting the free exercise thereof, in the light of its history and the evils it was designed forever to suppress, have been several times elaborated by the decisions of this Court prior to the application of the First Amendment to the states by the Fourteenth. The broad meaning given the Amendment by these earlier cases has been accepted by this Court in its decisions concerning an individual's religious freedom rendered since the Fourteenth Amendment was interpreted to make the prohibitions of the First applicable to state action abridging religious freedom. There is every reason to give the same application and broad interpretation to the "establishment of religion" clause.

The next paragraph of Justice Black's opinion is a very frequently quoted one and it unequivocally gives his interpretation of the Establishment Clause:

The "establishment of religion" clause of the First Amendment means at least this: Neither a state nor the Federal Government can set up a church. Neither can pass laws which aid one religion, aid all religions, or prefer one religion over another. Neither can force nor influence a person to go to or to remain away from church against his will or force him to profess a belief or disbelief in any religion. No person can be punished for entertaining or professing religious beliefs or disbeliefs, for church attendance or non-attendance. No tax in any amount, large or small, can be levied to support any religious activities or institutions, whatever they may be called, or whatever form they may adopt to teach or practice religion. Neither a state nor the Federal government can, openly or secretly, participate in the affairs of any religious organizations or groups or vice versa. In the words of Jefferson, the clause against establishment of religion by law was intended to erect "a wall of separation between church and State."

The standards by which the validity of the New Jersey statute must be judged are set forth as follows:

We must consider the New Jersey statute in accordance with the foregoing limitations imposed by the First Amendment. But we must not strike that state statute down if it is within the State's constitutional power even though it approaches the verge of that power. . . . New Jersey cannot consistently with the "establishment of religion" clause of the First Amendment contribute tax-raised funds to the support of any institution which teaches the tenets and faith of any church. On the other hand, other language of the amendment commands that New Jersey cannot hamper its citizens in the free exercise of their own religion. Consequently, it cannot exclude individual Catholics, Lutherans, Mohammedans, Baptists, Jews, Methodists, Non-believers, Presbyterians, or the members of any other faith, because of their faith or lack of it from receiving the benefits of public welfare legislation. While we do not mean to intimate that a state could not provide transportation only to children attending public schools, we must be careful, in protecting the citizens of New Jersey against state-established churches, to be sure that we do not inadvertently prohibit New Jersey from extending its general state law benefits to all its citizens without regard to their religious belief.

In concluding his opinion, Justice Black reaffirms the Court's adherence to the separation of church and state decreed by the terms of the First Amendment but concludes that the New Jersey statute does not violate constitutional requirements:

Measured by these standards, we cannot say that the First Amendment prohibits New Jersey from spending tax-raised funds to pay the bus fares of parochial school pupils as a part of a general program under which it pays the fares of pupils attending public and other schools. It is undoubtedly true that children are helped to get to church schools. There is even a possibility that some of the children might not be sent to the church schools if the parents were compelled to pay their children's bus fares out of their own pockets when transportation to a public school would have been paid for by the state. The same possibility exists where the state requires a local transit company to provide reduced fares to school children including those attending parochial schools, or where municipally owned transportation systems undertake to carry all school children free of charge. Moreover, state-paid policemen detailed to protect children going to and from church schools from the very real hazards of traffic, would serve much the same purpose and accomplish much the same result as state provisions intended to guarantee free transportation of a kind which the state deems to be best for the school children's welfare. And parents might refuse to risk their children to the serious danger of traffic accidents going to and from parochial schools, the approaches to which were not protected by policemen. Similarly, parents might be reluctant to permit their children to attend schools which the state had cut off from such general government services as ordinary police and fire protection, connections for sewage disposal, public highways and sidewalks. Of course, cutting off church schools from these services, so separate and so indisputably marked off from religious function, would make it far more difficult for the schools to operate. But such is obviously not the purpose of the First Amendment. That amendment requires the state to be neutral in its relations with groups of religious believers and non-believers; it does not require the state to be their adversary. State power is no more to be used so as to handicap religions than it is to favor them.

This Court has said that parents may, in the discharge of their duty under state compulsory education laws, send their children to a religious rather than a public school if the school meets the secular educational requirements which the state has the power to impose. See *Pierce* v. *Society of Sisters.* It appears that these parochial schools meet New Jersey's requirements. The State contributes no money to the schools. It does not support them. Its legislation, as applied, does no more than provide a general program to help parents get their children, regardless of their religion, safely and expeditiously to and from accredited schools.

The First Amendment has erected a wall between church and state. That wall must be kept high and impregnable. We could not approve the slightest breach. New Jersey has not breached it here.

DISSENTING OPINION OF JUSTICE JACKSON

Justice Jackson's dissenting opinion opened with a rather caustic comment on the nature of the majority opinion:

The Court's opinion marshals every argument in favor of state aid and puts the case in its most favorable light, but much of its reasoning confirms my conclusions that there are no good grounds upon which to support the present legislation. In fact, the undertones of the opinion, advocating complete and uncompromising separation of Church from State, seems utterly discordant with its conclusion yielding support to their commingling in educational matters. The case which irresistibly comes to mind as the most fitting precedent is that of Julia, who, according to Byron's reports, "whispering 'I will ne'er consent,'—consented."

Justice Jackson rejects the analogy drawn by the majority between the procedure here involved and the protection afforded by police and fire departments and objects to the fact that

Catholic schools, *as such*, are designated in the School Board's resolution, saying:

The Court sustains this legislation by assuming two deviations from the facts of this particular case; first, it assumes a state of facts the record does not support, and secondly, it refuses to consider facts which are inescapable on the record.

The Court concludes that this "legislation, as applied does no more than provide a general program to help parents get their children, regardless of their religion, safely and expeditiously to and from accredited schools," and it draws a comparison between "state provisions intended to guarantee free transportation" for school children with services such as police and fire protection, and implies that we are here dealing with "laws authorizing new types of public services. . . ." This hypothesis permeates the opinion. The facts will not bear that construction.

. . . What the Township does, and what the taxpayer complains of, is at stated intervals to reimburse parents for the fares paid, provided the children attend either public schools or Catholic church schools. . . .

In addition to thus assuming a type of service that does not exist, the Court also insists that we must close our eyes to a discrimination which does exist. The resolution which authorizes disbursement of this taxpayer's money limits reimbursement to those who attend public schools and Catholic schools. That is the way the Act is applied to this taxpayer.

The New Jersey Act in question makes the character of the school, not the needs of the children, determine the eligibility of parents to reimbursement. The Act permits payment for transportation to parochial schools or public schools but prohibits it to private schools operated in whole or in part for profit. . . . If all children of the state were objects of impartial solicitude, no reason is obvious for denying transportation reimbursement to students of this class, . . . Refusal to reimburse those who attend such schools is understandable only in the light of a purpose to aid the schools, because the state might well abstain from aiding a profit-making enterprise. Thus under the Act and resolution brought to us by this case, children are classified according to the schools they attend and are to be aided if they attend the public schools or private Catholic schools, and they are not allowed to be aided if they attend private secular schools or private religious schools of other faiths.

Of course, this case is not one of a Baptist or a Jew or an Episcopalian or a pupil of a private school complaining of discrimination. It is one of a taxpayer urging that he is being taxed for an unconstitutional purpose. I think he is entitled to have us consider the Act just as it is written. The statement by the New Jersey court that it holds the Legislature may authorize use of local funds "for the transportation of pupils to any school" . . . in view of the other constitutional views expressed, is not a holding that this Act authorizes transportation of *all* pupils to *all* schools. As applied to this taxpayer by the action he complains of, certainly the Act does not authorize reimbursement to those who choose any alternative to the public school except Catholic Church schools.

If we are to decide this case on the facts before us, our question is simply this: Is it constitutional to tax this complainant to pay the cost of carrying pupils to Church schools of one specified denomination?

The dissenting opinion next discusses the nature of Catholic parochial schools and their functions in part as follows:

It is no exaggeration to say that the whole historic conflict in temporal policy between the Catholic Church and non-Catholics come to a focus in their respective school policies. The Roman Catholic Church, counseled by experience in many ages and many lands and with all sorts of conditions and men, takes what, from the viewpoint of its own progress and the success of its mission, is a wise estimate of the importance of education to religion. It relies on early and indelible indoctrination in the faith and order of the Church by the word and example of persons consecrated to the task.

Our public school, if not a product of Protestantism, at least is more consistent with it than with the Catholic culture and scheme of values. It is a relatively recent development dating from about 1840. It is organized on the premise that secular education can be isolated from all religious teaching so that the school can inculcate all needed temporal knowledge and also maintain a strict and lofty neutrality as to religion. The assumption is that after the individual has been instructed in worldly wisdom he will be better fitted to choose his religion. Whether such a disjunction is possible, and if possible whether it is wise, are questions I need not try to answer.

The so-called "child benefit" theory is next discussed:

It is of no importance in this situation whether the beneficiary of this expenditure of tax-raised funds is primarily the parochial school and incidentally the pupil, or whether the aid is directly bestowed on the pupil with indirect benefits to the school. The State cannot maintain a Church and it can no more tax its citizens to furnish free carriage to those who attend a Church. The prohibition against establishment of religion cannot be circumvented by a subsidy, bonus, or reimbursement of expense to individuals for receiving religious instruction and indoctrination. . . .

The Court's holding is that this taxpayer has no grievance because the state has decided to make the reimbursement a public purpose and therefore we are bound to regard it as such. I agree that this Court has left, and always should leave to each state, great latitude in deciding for itself, in the light of its own conditions, what shall be public purposes in its scheme of things. It may socialize utilities and economic enterprises and make taxpayers' business out of what conventionally had been private business. It may make public business of individual welfare, health, education, entertainment or security. But it cannot make public business of religious worship or instruction, or of attendance at religious institutions of any character. There is no answer to the proposition, more fully expounded by Mr. Justice Rutledge, that the effect of the religious freedom Amendment to our Constitution was to take every form of propagation of religion out of the realm of things which could directly or indirectly be made public business and thereby be supported in whole or in part at taxpayers' expense. . . .

Justice Jackson then comments on the attitude of religious groups concerning the provisions of the First Amendment:

This policy of our Federal Constitution has never been wholly pleasing to most religious groups. They all are quick to invoke its protections; they are all irked when they feel its restraints. . . .

But we cannot have it both ways. Religious teaching cannot be a private affair when the state seeks to impose regulations which infringe on it indirectly, and a public affair when it comes to taxing citizens of one faith to aid another, or those of no faith to aid all. If these principles seem harsh in prohibiting aid to Catholic education, it must not be forgotten that it is the same Constitution that alone assures Catholics the right to maintain these schools at all when predominant local sentiment would forbid them. *Pierce* v. *Society of Sisters,* . . .

The opinion concludes:

But in any event, the great purposes of the Constitution do not depend on the approval or convenience of those they restrain. I cannot read the story of the struggle to separate political from ecclesiastical affairs, well summarized in the opinion of Mr. Justice Rutledge in which I generally concur, without a conviction that the Court today is unconsciously giving the clock's hands a backward turn.

JUSTICE RUTLEDGE DISSENTS

Justice Rutledge wrote a lengthy and exhaustive opinion which he opened by expressing distress at the implications of the majority ruling:

. . . Neither so high nor so impregnable today as yesterday is the wall raised between church and state by Virginia's great statute of religious freedom and the First Amendment, now made applicable to all the states by the Fourteenth. New Jersey's statute sustained is the first, if indeed it is not the second breach to be made by this Court's action. That a third, and a fourth, and still others will be attempted, we may be sure. For just as *Cochran* v. *Board of Education,* has opened the way by oblique ruling for this decision, so will the two make wider the breach for a third. Thus with time the most solid freedom steadily gives way before continuing corrosive decision.

First discussed is the fallacy of the argument that the Establishment Clause refers only to the establishment of a state church:

Not simply an established church, but any law respecting an establishment of religion is forbidden. The Amendment was broadly but not loosely phrased. . . .

The Amendment's purpose was not to strike merely at the official establishment of a single sect, creed or religion, outlawing only a formal relation such as had prevailed in England and some of the colonies. Necessarily it was to uproot all such relationships. But the object was broader than separating church and state in this narrow sense. It was to create a complete and permanent separation of the spheres of religious activity and civil authority by comprehensively forbidding every form of public aid or support for religion. . . .

"Religion" has the same broad significance in the twin prohibition concerning an "establishment." The Amendment was not duplicitous. "Religion" and "establishment" were not used in any formal or technical sense. The prohibition broadly forbids state support, financial or other, of religion in any guise, form or degree. It outlaws all use of public funds for religious purposes.

In a rather lengthy section of his opinion Justice Rutledge gives a lucid picture of the historical background of the First Amendment. Because this history is so basic to an adequate understanding of the language used in that Amendment, this portion of the opinion is given at length:

No provision of the Constitution is more closely tied to or given content by its generating history than the religious clause of the First Amendment. It is at once the refined product and the terse summation of that history. The history includes not only Madison's authorship and the proceedings before the First Congress, but also the long and intensive struggle for religious freedom in America, more especially in Virginia, of which the Amendment was the direct culmination. In the documents of the times, particularly of Madison, who was the leader in the Virginia struggle before he became the Amendment's sponsor, but also in the writings of Jefferson and others and in the issues which engendered them is to be found irrefutable confirmation of the Amendment's sweeping content.

For Madison, as also for Jefferson, religious freedom was the crux of the struggle for freedom in general. . . . Madison was co-author with George Mason of the religious clause in Virginia's great Declaration of Rights in 1776. He is credited with changing it from a mere statement of the principle of tolerance to the first official legislative pronouncement that freedom of conscience and religion are inherent rights of the individual. He sought also to have the Declaration expressly condemn the existing Virginia establishment. But the forces supporting it were then too strong.

Accordingly Madison yielded on this phase but not for long. At once he resumed the fight, continuing it before succeeding legislative sessions. As a member of the General Assembly in 1779 he threw his full weight behind Jefferson's historic Bill for Establishing Religious Freedom. That bill was a prime phase of Jefferson's broad program of democratic reform undertaken on his return from the Continental Congress in 1776 and submitted for the General Assembly's consideration in 1779 as his proposed revised Virginia code. With Jefferson's departure for Europe in 1784, Madison became the Bill's prime sponsor. Enactment failed in successive legislatures from its introduction in June, 1779, until its adoption in January, 1786. But during all this time the fight for religious freedom moved forward in Virginia on various fronts with growing intensity. Madison led throughout, against Patrick Henry's powerful opposing leadership until Henry was elected governor in November, 1784.

The climax came in the legislative struggle of 1784–1785 over the Assessment Bill. . . . This was nothing more nor less than a taxing measure for the support of religion, designed to revive the payment of tithes suspended since 1777. So long as it singled out a particular sect for preference it incurred the active and general hostility of dissentient groups. It was broadened to include them, with the result that some subsided temporarily in their opposition. As altered, the bill gave to each taxpayer the privilege of designating which church should receive his share of the tax. In default of designation the legislature applied it to pious uses. But what is of the utmost significance here, "in its final form the bill left the taxpayer the option of giving his tax to education."

Madison was unyielding at all times, opposing with all his vigor the general and nondiscriminatory as he had the earlier particular and discriminatory assessments proposed. The modified Assessment

Bill passed second reading in December, 1784, and was all but enacted. Madison and his followers, however, maneuvered deferment of final consideration until November, 1785. And before the Assembly reconvened in the fall he issued his historic Memorial and Remonstrance.

This is Madison's complete, though not his only, interpretation of religious liberty. It is a broadside attack upon all forms of "establishment" of religion, both general and particular, nondiscriminatory or selective. Reflecting not only the many legislative conflicts over the Assessment Bill and the Bill for Establishing Religious Freedom but also, for example, the struggles for religious incorporations and the continued maintenance of the glebes, the Remonstrance is at once the most concise and the most accurate statement of the views of the First Amendment's author concerning what is "an establishment of religion." Because it behooves us in the dimming distance of time not to lose sight of what he and his co-workers had in mind when, by a single sweeping stroke of the pen, they forbade an establishment of religion and secured its free exercise, the text of the Remonstrance is appended at the end of this opinion for its wider current reference, together with a copy of the bill against which it was directed.

The Remonstrance, stirring up a storm of popular protest, killed the Assessment Bill. It collapsed in committee shortly before Christmas, 1785. With this, the way was cleared at last for enactment of Jefferson's Bill for Establishing Religious Freedom. Madison promptly drove it through in January of 1786, seven years from the time it was first introduced. This dual victory substantially ended the fight over establishments, settling the issue against them. . . .

The next year Madison became a member of the Constitutional Convention. Its work done, he fought valiantly to secure the ratification of its great product in Virginia as elsewhere, and nowhere else more effectively. Madison was certain in his own mind that under the Constitution "there is not a shadow of right in the general government to intermeddle with religion" and that "this subject is, for the honor of America, perfectly free and unshackled. The government has no jurisdiction over it. . . ." Nevertheless he pledged that he would work for a Bill of Rights, including a specific

guaranty of religious freedom, and Virginia, with other states, ratified the Constitution on this assurance.

Ratification thus accomplished, Madison was sent to the first
Congress. There he went at once about performing his pledge to
establish freedom for the nation as he had done in Virginia. Within
a little more than three years from his legislative victory at home
he had proposed and secured the submission and ratification of the
First Amendment as the first article of our Bill of Rights.

All the great instruments of the Virginia struggle for religious
liberty thus became warp and woof of our constitutional tradition,
not simply by the course of history, but by the common unifying
force of Madison's life, thought and sponsorship. He epitomized
the whole of that tradition in the Amendment's compact, but
nonetheless comprehensive, phrasing.

As the Remonstrance discloses throughout, Madison opposed
every form and degree of official relation between religion and
civil authority. For him religion was a wholly private matter beyond the scope of civil power either to restrain or to support. Denial or abridgment of religious freedom was a violation of rights
both of conscience and of natural equality. State aid was no less
obnoxious or destructive to freedom and to religion itself than other
forms of state interference. "Establishment" and "free exercise"
were correlative and coextensive ideas, representing only different
facets of the single great and fundamental freedom. The Remonstrance, following the Virginia statute's example, referred to the
history of religious conflicts and the effects of all sorts of establishments, current and historical, to suppress religion's free exercise.
With Jefferson, Madison believed that to tolerate any fragment of
establishment would be by so much to perpetuate restraint upon
that freedom. Hence he sought to tear out the institution not
partially but root and branch, and to bar its return forever.

In no phase was he more unrelentingly absolute than in opposing state support or aid by taxation. Not even "three pence" contribution was thus to be exacted from any citizen for such a purpose.
. . . Tithes had been the lifeblood of establishment before and
after other compulsions disappeared. Madison and his co-workers
made no exceptions or abridgments to the complete separation they
created. (Their objection was not to small tithes.) It was to any

tithes whatsoever. "If it were lawful to impose a small tax for religion, the admission would pave the way for oppressive levies." Not the amount but "the principle of assessment was wrong." And the principle was as much to prevent "the interference of law in religion" as to restrain religious intervention in political matters. In this field the authors of our freedom would not tolerate "the first experiment on our liberties" or "wait till usurped power had strengthened itself by exercise and entangled the question in precedents. . . ." Nor should we.

In view of this history no further proof is needed that the Amendment forbids any appropriation, large or small, from public funds to aid or support any and all religious exercises. But if more were called for, the debates in the First Congress and this Court's consistent expressions, whenever it has touched on the matter directly, supply it.

By contrast with the Virginia history, the congressional debates on consideration of the Amendment reveal only sparse discussion, reflecting the fact that the essential issues had been settled. Indeed the matter had become so well understood as to have been taken for granted in all but formal phrasing. Hence, the only enlightening reference shows concern, not to preserve any power to use public funds in aid of religion, but to prevent the Amendment from outlawing private gifts inadvertently by virtue of the breadth of its wording. . . .

The "public function" concept is next discussed:

But we are told that the New Jersey statute is valid in its present application because the appropriation is for a public, not private purpose, namely, the promotion of education, and the majority accept this idea in the conclusion that all we have here is "public welfare legislation." . . .

If the fact alone be determinative that religious schools are engaged in education, thus promoting the general and individual welfare, together with the legislature's decision that the payment of public moneys for their aid makes their work a public function, then I can see no possible basis, except one of dubious legislative policy, for the state's refusal to make full appropriation for support of private, religious schools, just as is done for public instruction. . . .

Of course paying the cost of transportation promotes the general cause of education and the welfare of the individual. So does paying all other items of educational expense. . . .

These things are beside the real question. They have no materiality except to obscure the all-pervading, inescapable issue. . . . Stripped of its religious phase, the case presents no substantial federal question. . . .

. . . To say that New Jersey's appropriation and her use of the power of taxation for raising the funds appropriated are not for public purposes, but for private ends, is to say that they are for the support of religion and religious teaching. Conversely, to say that they are for public purposes is to say that they are not for religious ones.

This is precisely for the reason that education which includes religious training and teaching, and its support, have been made matters of private, not public, right and function by the very terms of the First Amendment. That is the effect not only in its guaranty of religion's free exercise, but also in the prohibition of establishments. It was on this basis of the private character of the function of religious education that this Court held parents entitled to send their children to private, religious schools. *Pierce* v. *Society of Sisters.* Now it declares in effect that the appropriation of public funds to defray part of the cost of attending those schools is for a public purpose. If so, I do not understand why the state cannot go farther or why this case approaches the verge of its power.

In truth this view contradicts the whole purpose and effect of the First Amendment as heretofore conceived. . . .

It is not because religious teaching does not promote the public or the individual's welfare, but because neither is furthered when the state promotes religious education, that the Constitution forbids it to do so. Both legislatures and courts are bound by that distinction. . . .

Justice Rutledge concludes his opinion by saying:

No one conscious of religious values can be unsympathetic toward the burden which our constitutional separation puts on parents who desire religious instruction mixed with secular for their children. They pay taxes for others' children's education, at the same time the added cost of instruction for their own. Nor can one happily see benefits denied to children which others receive, because in conscience they or their parents for them desire a different kind of training others do not demand.

But if those feelings should prevail, there would be an end to our historic constitutional policy and command. No more unjust or discriminatory in fact is it to deny attendants at religious schools the cost of their transportation than to deny them tuitions, sustenance for their teachers, or any other educational expense which others receive at public cost. Hardship in fact there is which none can blink. But, for assuring to those who undergo it the greater, the most comprehensive freedom, it is one written by design and firm intent into our basic law.

Of course discrimination in the legal sense does not exist. The child attending the religious school has the same right as any other to attend the public school. But he foregoes exercising it because the same guaranty which assures this freedom forbids the public school or any agency of the state to give or aid him in securing the religious instruction he seeks.

Were he to accept the common school, he would be the first to protest the teaching there of any creed or faith not his own. And it is precisely for the reason that their atmosphere is wholly secular that children are not sent to public schools under the *Pierce* doctrine. But that is a constitutional necessity, because we have staked the very existence of our country on the faith that complete separation between the state and religion is best for the state and best for religion. . . .

That policy necessarily entails hardship upon persons who forego the right to educational advantages the state can supply in order to secure others it is precluded from giving. Indeed this may hamper the parent and the child forced by conscience to that choice. But it does not make the state unneutral to withhold what the Constitution forbids it to give. On the contrary it is only by observing the prohibition rigidly that the state can maintain its neutrality and avoid partisanship in the dissensions inevitable when sect opposes sect over demands for public moneys to further religious education, teaching or training in any form or degree, directly or indirectly. . . .

The problem then cannot be cast in terms of legal discrimination or its absence. This would be true, even though the state in giving aid should treat all religious instruction alike. Thus, if the present statute and its application were shown to apply equally to all religious schools of whatever faith, yet in the light of our tradition it could not stand. For then the adherent of one creed still would pay for the support of another, the childless taxpayer with others more fortunate. Then too, there would seem to be no bar to making appropriations for transportation and other expenses of children attending public or other secular schools, after hours in separate places and classes for their exclusively religious instruction. The person who embraces no creed also would be forced to pay for teaching what he does not believe. Again, it was the furnishing of "contributions of money for the propagation of opinions which he disbelieves" that the fathers outlawed. That consequence and effect are not removed by multiplying to all-inclusiveness the sects for which support is exacted. The Constitution requires, not comprehensive identification of state with religion, but complete separation.

Two great drives are constantly in motion to abridge, in the name of education, the complete division of religion and civil authority which our forefathers made. One is to introduce religious education and observances into the public schools. The other, to obtain public funds for the aid and support of various private religious schools. . . . In my opinion both avenues were closed by the Constitution. Neither should be opened by this Court. The matter is not one of quantity, to be measured by the amount of money expended. Now as in Madison's day it is one of principle, to keep separate the separate spheres as the First Amendment drew them; to prevent the first experiment upon our liberties; and to keep the question from becoming entangled in corrosive precedents. We should not be less strict to keep strong and untarnished the one side of the shield of religious freedom than we have been of the other.

The judgment should be reversed.

The ruling in this case was that under the child-benefit theory, a state could arrange for the reimbursement of transportation expenses incurred by parents in sending their children to a private school. The Court decided that such a payment was not a violation of the Establishment Clause of the First Amendment.

SUMMARY

1. In *Cochran v. Louisiana* the Supreme Court upheld the validity of a Louisiana statute providing for the use of tax moneys to furnish school textbooks not only to public school pupils but to pupils of nonpublic schools as well. The statute was attacked as taking private property for private use as prohibited by the Fourteenth Amendment. The First Amendment was not mentioned. The statute was upheld on the theory that the expenditure was for the benefit of all children and not for the benefit of any school.

2. In *Everson v. Board of Education* (1947) a New Jersey statute permitting the use of tax moneys to reimburse parents for the cost of transporting their children to nonprofit private schools as well as to public schools, was under attack. It was urged that the statute was in violation of the Establishment Clause of the First Amendment.

3. The Supreme Court of the United States in a 5–4 decision affirmed a holding of the New Jersey Court of Appeals upholding the validity of the statute on the ground that no aid was being given by this law to any religious institution but only to school children and their parents. However, strong language was used to stress the necessity of not breaching the "wall between church and state" erected by the First Amendment.

4. Justice Jackson in his dissenting opinion found the Court's advocacy of a complete and uncompromising separation of church and state inconsistent with its declaration of the validity of the acts complained of. He labelled the effect of the decision as "unconsciously giving the clock's hands a backward turn."

5. Justice Rutledge, in a lengthy opinion, reviewed the history of the First Amendment and concluded that this history showed that it was intended that the Amendment forbid any appropriation whatsoever to aid religious exercises. He stated that the aid in question was such a prohibited use of public property.

CHAPTER 6

RELIGIOUS INSTRUCTION
DURING SCHOOL HOURS

To what extent may public schools constitutionally participate in, or give aid to plans for providing religious instruction to children during school hours? In the two cases excerpted and commented upon in this chapter, this question is answered by the Supreme Court of the United States.

In the *McCollum* case the Court was not in full agreement, but eight of the Justices (Vinson, Black, Frankfurter, Douglas, Murphy, Jackson, Rutledge, and Burton) arrived at the conclusion that the school's practices were unconstitutional under the First and Fourteenth Amendments. Justice Reed alone dissented. When the *Zorach* case was decided in 1952, four years later, Justices Clark and Minton had replaced Justices Murphy and Rutledge. Now the Court was sharply divided on the issue of whether or not the *Zorach* case was distinguishable from the *McCollum* case. The majority decided that there was a real difference in the facts presented and held that this case in no way overruled the previous holding in the *McCollum* case.

ILLINOIS ex. rel. McCOLLUM v. *BOARD OF EDUCATION SCHOOL DISTRICT NO. 71, CHAMPAIGN COUNTY, ILLINOIS, et al.*[1]

In this case the question was whether the release of public school pupils from their classes to attend sectarian religious instruction during the school day was permissible under the terms of the Establishment Clause of the First Amendment.

This case was an appeal from a 1947 decision by the Supreme Court of Illinois. In the decision of that court the facts involved were stated as follows:

The record discloses that in the fall of 1940 the Champaign Council of Religious Education, a voluntary association of Jewish, Roman Catholic, and Protestant faiths, was formed. They immediately sought and secured from the Board of Education . . . permission to offer classes in religious instruction in grades four through nine. Qualified instructors, all materials and books . . . were to be furnished at the expense of the council. Admission to the classes was to be allowed only upon the express written request of parents, and then only to classes designated by the parents. They were to be excused by the board from attendance in the grade schools for 30 minutes and from the junior high school for a period of 45 minutes each week for participation in the religious education classes. Classes were to be scheduled so as not to interfere with the regular public school classes after consultation with the public school teachers. Each faith . . . was to have its separate instructional class and no expense . . . was to be borne by the board. Additional groups were to be freely permitted to participate upon the same terms. Lesson materials and curriculum were to be selected by a committee representative of all groups participating and in a manner to avoid any offensive, doctrinal, dogmatic, or sectarian teaching. It is apparent the teaching was to be the content of the Bible without interpretation or attempt at influencing belief in the doctrines or creeds of any church.

[1] 333 U.S. 203. Decided March 8, 1948.

The classes in question were held in the public school buildings. The son of the plaintiff did not participate in the religious instruction. During one semester he was the only pupil abstaining and during another he was one of two nonparticipants.

THE OPINION OF THE COURT

The opinion of the Court was delivered by Justice Black, who stated the issue of the case as follows:

This case relates to the power of a State to utilize its tax-supported public school system in aid of religious instruction in so far as that power may be restricted by the First and Fourteenth Amendments to the Federal Constitution.

The opinion continues:

The appellant, Vashti McCollum, began this action . . . against the Champaign Board of Education in the Circuit Court of Champaign County, Illinois. Her asserted interest was that of a resident and taxpayer of Champaign and of a parent whose child was then enrolled in the Champaign public schools. Illinois has a compulsory education law, . . . District boards of education are given general supervisory powers over the use of the public school buildings within the school districts.

Appellant's petition . . . alleged that religious teachers, employed by private religious groups, were permitted to come weekly into the school buildings during the regular hours set apart for secular teaching, and then and there for a period of thirty minutes substitute their religious teaching for the secular education provided under the compulsory education law. The petitioner charged that this joint public-school religious-group program violated the First and Fourteenth Amendments to the United States Constitution. The prayer of her petition was that the Board of Education be ordered to "adopt and enforce rules and regulations prohibiting all instruction in and teaching of religious education in all public schools in Champaign School District Number 71, . . . and in all public school houses and buildings in said district when occupied by public schools."

After disposing of three technical points raised, the Court gives a recital of the facts involved, including the following footnote:

The State Supreme Court said: "The record further discloses that the teachers conducting the religious classes were not teachers in the public schools but were subject to the approval and supervision of the superintendent . . ." The trial court found: "Before any faith or other group may obtain permission from the defendant for the similar, free and equal use of rooms in the public school buildings said faith or group must make application to the superintendent of schools of said School District Number 71, who in turn will determine whether or not it is practical for said group to teach in said school system." The president of the local school board testified: ". . . The Protestants would have one group and the Catholics another and each would be given a room where they would have the class and we would go along with the plan of the religious people. They were all to be treated alike, with the understanding that the teachers they would bring into the school were approved by the superintendent . . . The superintendent was the last word so far as the individual was concerned . . ."

After stating these facts, the following unequivocal language is used:

The foregoing facts, without reference to others that appear in the record, show the use of tax-supported property for religious instruction and the close cooperation between the school authorities and the religious council in promoting religious education. The operation of the State's compulsory education system thus assists and is integrated with the program of religious instruction carried on by separate religious sects. Pupils compelled by law to go to school for secular education are released in part from their legal duty upon the condition that they attend the religious classes. This is beyond all question a utilization of the tax-established and tax-supported public school system to aid religious groups to spread their faith. And it falls squarely under the ban of the First Amendment (made applicable to the States by the Fourteenth) as we interpreted it in *Everson v. Board of Education.* There we said: "Neither a state nor the Federal Government can set up a church. Neither can pass laws which aid one religion, aid all religions, or prefer one religion over another. Neither can force or influence a person to go to or to remain away from church against his will or force him to profess a belief or disbelief in any religion. No person can be punished for entertaining or professing religious beliefs or disbeliefs, for church attendance or non-attendance. No tax in any amount, large or small, can be levied to support any religious activities or institutions, whatever they may be called, or whatever form they may adopt to teach or practice religion. Neither a State nor the Federal Government can, openly or secretly, participate in the affairs of any religious organizations or groups and vice versa. In the words of Jefferson, the clause against the establishment of religion by law was intended to erect "a wall of separation between church and State."

The opinion quotes the following language from the dissenting opinion in the *Everson* case:

The problem then cannot be cast in terms of legal discrimination or its absence. This would be true, even though the state in giving aid should treat all religious instruction alike. . . . Again, it was the furnishing of "contributions of money for the propagation of opinions which he disbelieves" that the fathers outlawed. That consequence and effect are not removed by multiplying to all-inclusiveness the sects for which support is exacted. The Constitution requires, not comprehensive identification of state with religion, but complete separation. *Everson v. Board of Education.*

In view of this history no further proof is needed that the Amendment forbids any appropriation, large or small, from public funds to aid or support any or all religious exercises. . . . Legislatures are free to make, and courts to sustain, appropriations only when it can be found that in fact they do not aid, promote, encourage, or sustain religious teaching or observances, be the amount large or small. *Everson v. Board of Education.*

The quotation of these passages from a dissenting opinion is an excellent illustration of the weight given the views expressed in such decisions by the Court in its future deliberations.

The opinion continues:

The majority in the *Everson* case and the minority agreed that the First Amendment's language, properly interpreted, had erected a wall of separation between Church and State. They disagreed as to the facts shown by the record and as to the proper application of the First Amendment's language to those facts.

Recognizing that the Illinois program is barred by the First and Fourteenth Amendments if we adhere to the views expressed both by the majority and the minority in the *Everson* case, counsel for the respondents challenge those views as dicta and urge that we reconsider and repudiate them.

This argument rests upon the theory that since the Court's holding in *Everson* was that the acts complained of (see Chapter 5) did not violate the Establishment Clause of the First Amendment, any definition of that clause was not necessary to the decision. Such extraneous matter in an opinion is referred to as obiter dicta (see Chapter 1) and is not strictly binding upon the Court in its future decisions.

Continuing to describe the school district's arguments the Court states:

They argue that historically the First Amendment was intended to forbid only government preference of one religion over another, not an impartial governmental assistance of all religions. In addition they ask that we distinguish or overrule our holding in the *Everson* case that the Fourteenth Amendment made the "establishment of religion" clause of the First Amendment applicable as a prohibition against the States.

The Court rejects these arguments, saying:

After giving full consideration to the arguments presented we are unable to accept either of these contentions.

To hold that a state cannot consistently with the First and Fourteenth Amendments utilize its public school system to aid any or all religious faiths or sects in the dissemination of their doctrines and ideas does not, as counsel urge, manifest a governmental hostility to religion or religious teachings. A manifestation of such hostility would be at war with our national tradition as embodied in the First Amendment's guaranty of the free exercise of religion. For the First Amendment rests upon the premise that both religion and government can best work to achieve their lofty aims if each is left free from the other within its respective sphere. Or, as we said in the *Everson* case, the First Amendment has erected a wall between Church and State which must be kept high and impregnable.

Here not only are the State's tax-supported public school buildings used for the dissemination of religious doctrines. The State also affords sectarian groups an invaluable aid in that it helps to provide pupils for their religious classes through the use of the State's compulsory public school machinery. This is not separation of Church and State.

CONCURRING OPINION

Justices Rutledge and Burton joined in the Court's opinion as delivered by Justice Black. They also joined with Justice Jackson in a concurring opinion written by Justice Frankfurter. In this opinion the history of the philosophy underlying the First Amendment was examined in detail. The opinion commenced:

We dissented in *Everson v. Board of Education*, 330 U.S. 1, because in our view the Constitutional principle requiring separation of Church and State compelled invalidation of the ordinance sustained by the majority. Illinois has here authorized the commingling of sectarian with secular instruction in the public schools. The Constitution of the United States forbids this.

This case, in the light of the *Everson* decision, demonstrates anew that the mere formulation of a relevant Constitutional principle is the beginning of the solution of a problem, not its answer.

This is so because the meaning of a spacious conception like that of the separation of Church from State is unfolded as appeal is made to the principle from case to case. We are all agreed that the First and Fourteenth Amendments have a secular reach far more penetrating in the conduct of Government than merely to forbid an "established church." But agreement, in the abstract, that the First Amendment was designed to erect a "wall of separation between Church and State," does not preclude a clash of views as to what the wall separates. . . . We cannot illuminatingly apply the "wall-of-separation" metaphor until we have considered the relevant history of religious education in America, the place of the "released time" movement in that history, and its precise manifestation in the case before us.

To understand the particular program now before us as a conscientious attempt to accommodate the allowable functions of Government and the special concerns of the Church within the framework of our Constitution and with due regard to the kind of society for which it was designed, we must put this Champaign program of 1940 in its historic setting. Traditionally, organized education in the Western world was Church education. . . . Even in the Protestant countries, where there was a less close identification of Church and State, the basis of education was largely the Bible, and its chief purpose inculcation of piety. . . .

The evolution of colonial education, largely in the service of religion, into the public school system of today is the story of changing conceptions regarding the American democratic society, of the functions of State-maintained education in such a society, and of the role therein of the free exercise of religion by the people. The modern public school derived from a philosophy of freedom reflected in the First Amendment. It is appropriate to recall that the Remonstrance of James Madison, an event basic in the history of religious liberty, was called forth by a proposal which involved support to religious education. . . . As the momentum for popular education increased and in turn evoked strong claims for State support of religious education, contests not unlike that which in Virginia had produced Madison's Remonstrance appeared in various forms in other States. . . . The upshot of these controversies, often long and fierce, is fairly summarized by saying that long before the Fourteenth Amendment subjected the States to new limitations, the prohibition of furtherance by the State of religious instruction became the guiding principle, in law and feeling, of the American people. . . .

Separation in the field of education, then, was not imposed upon unwilling States by force of superior law. . . . the Fourteenth Amendment merely reflected a principle then dominant in our national life. To the extent that the Constitution made it binding upon the States, the basis of the restriction is the whole experience of our people. Zealous watchfulness against fusion of secular and religious activities by Government itself, through any of its instruments but especially through its educational agencies, was the democratic response of the American community to the particular needs of a young and growing nation, unique in the composition of its people. . . .

It is pertinent to remind that the establishment of this principle of Separation in the field of education was not due to any decline in the religious beliefs of the people. Horace Mann was a devout Christian, and the deep religious feeling of James Madison is stamped upon the Remonstrance. The secular public school did not imply indifference to the basic role of religion in the life of the people, nor rejection of religious education as a means of fostering it. The claims of religion were not minimized by refusing to make the public schools agencies for their assertion. The non-sectarian or secular public school was the means of reconciling freedom in general with religious freedom. The sharp confinement of the public schools to secular education was a recognition of the need of a democratic society to educate its children, insofar as the State undertook to do so, in an atmosphere free from pressures in a realm in which pressures are most resisted and where conflicts are most easily and most bitterly engendered. Designed to serve as perhaps the most powerful agency for promoting cohesion among a heterogeneous democratic people, the public school must keep scrupulously free from entanglement in the strife of sects. The preservation of the community from divisive conflicts, of Government from irreconcilable pressures by religious groups, of religion from censorship and coercion however subtly exercised, requires strict confinement of the State to instruction other than religious, leaving to the individual's church and home, indoctrination in the faith of his choice.

This development of the public school as a symbol of our secular unity was not a sudden achievement nor attained without violent conflict. While in small communities of comparatively homogeneous religious beliefs, the need for absolute separation presented no urgencies, elsewhere the growth of the secular school encountered the resistance of feeling strongly engaged against it. But the inevitability of such attempts is the very reason for Constitutional provisions primarily concerned with the protection of minority groups. And such sects are shifting groups, varying from time to time, and place to place, thus representing in their totality the common interest of the nation.

Enough has been said to indicate that we are dealing not with a full-blown principle, nor one having the definiteness of a surveyor's metes and bounds. But by 1875 the separation of public education from Church entanglements, of the State from the teaching of religion, was firmly established in the consciousness of the nation.

Prohibition of the commingling of sectarian and secular instruction in the public school is of course only half the story. A religious people was naturally concerned about the part of the child's education entrusted "to the family altar, the church, and the private school." The promotion of religious education took many forms. Laboring under financial difficulties and exercising only persuasive authority, various denominations felt handicapped in their task of religious education. Abortive attempts were therefore frequently made to obtain public funds for religious schools. But the major efforts of religious inculcation were a recognition of the principle of Separation by the establishment of church schools privately supported. Parochial schools were maintained by various denominations. These, however, were often beset by serious handicaps, financial and otherwise, so that the religious aims which they represented found other directions.

The opinion now reviews the history of the "released-time" movement:

There were experiments with vacation schools, with Saturday as well as Sunday schools. They all fell short of their purpose. It was urged that by appearing to make religion a one-day-a-week matter, the Sunday school, which acquired national acceptance, tended to relegate the child's religious education, and thereby his religion, to a minor role not unlike the enforced piano lesson.

Out of these inadequate efforts evolved the week-day church school, held on one or more afternoons a week after the close of the public school. But children continued to be children; they wanted to play when school was out, particularly when other children were free to do so. Church leaders decided that if the week-day church school was to succeed, a way had to be found to give the child his religious education during what the child conceived to be his "business hours."

The initiation of the movement may fairly be attributed to Dr. George U. Wenner. The underlying assumption of his proposal, made at the Interfaith Conference on Federation held in New York City in 1905, was that the public school unduly monopolized the child's time and that the churches were entitled to their share of it. This, the schools should "release." Accordingly, the Federation, citing the example of the Third Republic of France, urged that upon the request of their parents children be excused from public school on Wednesday afternoon, so that the churches could provide "Sunday school on Wednesday." This was to be carried out on church premises under church authority. Those not desiring to attend church schools would continue their normal classes. Lest these public school classes unfairly compete with the church education, it was requested that the school authorities refrain from scheduling courses or activities of compelling interest or importance.

The proposal aroused considerable opposition and it took another decade for a "released time" scheme to become part of a public school system. Gary, Indiana, inaugurated the movement. At a time when industrial expansion strained the communal facilities of the city, Superintendent of Schools Wirt suggested a fuller use of the school buildings. Building on theories which had become more or less current, he also urged that education was more than instruction in the classroom. The school was only one of several educational agencies. The library, the playground, the home, the church, all have their function in the child's proper unfolding. Accordingly, Wirt's plan sought to rotate the schedules of the children during the school-day so that some were in class, others were in the library, still others in the playground. And some, he suggested to the leading ministers of the City, might be released to attend religious classes if the churches of the City cooperated and provided them. They did, in 1914, and thus was "released time" begun. The religious teaching was held on church premises and the public schools had no hand in the conduct of these church schools. They did not supervise the choice of instructors or the subject matter taught. Nor did they assume responsibility for the attendance, conduct or achievement of the child in a church school; and he received no credit for it. The period of attendance in the religious schools would otherwise have been a play period for the child, with the result that the arrangement did not cut into public school instruction or truly affect the activities or feelings of the children who did not attend the church schools.

From such a beginning "released time" has attained substantial proportions. In 1914–15, under the Gary program, 619 pupils left the public schools for the church schools during one period a week. According to responsible figures almost 2,000,000 in some 2,200 communities participated in "released time" programs during 1947. A movement of such scope indicates the importance of the problem to which the "released time" programs are directed. But to the extent that aspects of these programs are open to Constitutional objection, the more extensively the movement operates, the more ominous the breaches in the wall of separation.

After completing this historical review, the opinion gives a broad hint of things to come. We now know, by virtue of hindsight, that these hints were to be borne out in the Zorach case.

Of course, "released time" as a generalized conception, undefined by differentiating particularities, is not an issue for Constitutional adjudication. Local programs differ from each other in many and crucial respects. Some "released time" classes are under separate denominational auspices, others are conducted jointly by several denominations, often embracing all the religious affiliations of a community. Some classes in religion teach a limited sectarianism; others emphasize democracy, unity and spiritual values not anchored in a particular creed. Insofar as these are manifestations merely of the free exercise of religion, they are quite outside the scope of judicial concern, except insofar as the Court may be called upon to protect the right of religious freedom. It is only when challenge is made to the share that the public schools have in the execution of a particular "released time" program that close judicial scrutiny is demanded of the exact relation between the religious instruction and the public educational system in the specific situation before the Court.

In a footnote examples are given of ways in which various released-time programs operate:

Respects in which programs differ include, for example, the amount of supervision by the public school of attendance and performance in the religious class, of the course of study, of the selection of teachers; methods of enrollment and dismissal from the secular classes; the amount of school time devoted to operation of the program; the extent to which school property and administrative machinery are involved; the effect on the public school program of the introduction of "released time"; the proportion of students who seek to be excused; the effect of the program on non-participants; the amount and nature of the publicity for the program in the public schools.

Justice Frankfurter's opinion continues:

The substantial differences among arrangements lumped together as "released time" emphasize the importance of detailed analysis of the facts to which the Constitutional test of Separation is to be applied. How does "released time" operate in Champaign? Public school teachers distribute to their pupils cards supplied by church groups, so that the parents may indicate whether they desire religious instruction for their children. For those desiring it, religious classes are conducted in the regular classrooms of the public schools by teachers of religion paid by the churches and appointed by them, but, as the State court found, "subject to the approval and supervision of the superintendent." The courses do not profess to give secular instruction in subjects concerning religion. Their candid purpose is sectarian teaching. While a child can go to any of the religious classes offered, a particular sect wishing a teacher for its devotees requires the permission of the school superintendent "who in turn will determine whether or not it is practical for said group to teach in said school system." If no provision is made for religious instruction in the particular faith of a child, or if for other reasons the child is not enrolled in any of the offered classes, he is required to attend a regular school class, or a study period during which he is often left to his own devices. Reports of attendance in the religious classes are submitted by the religious instructor to the school authorities, and the child who fails to attend is presumably deemed a truant.

Religious education so conducted on school time and property is patently woven into the working scheme of the school. The Champaign arrangement thus presents powerful elements of inherent pressure by the school system in the interests of religious sects. The fact that this power has not been used to discriminate is beside the point. Separation is a requirement to abstain from fusing functions of Government and of religious sects, not merely to treat them all equally. That a child is offered an alternative may reduce the constraint; it does not eliminate the operation of influence by the school in matters sacred to conscience and outside the school's domain. The law of imitation operates, and non-conformity is not an outstanding characteristic of children. The result is an obvious pressure upon children to attend. Again, while the Champaign school population represents only a fraction of the more than two hundred and fifty sects of the nation, not even all the practicing sects in Champaign are willing or able to provide religious instruction. The children belonging to these non-participating sects will thus have inculcated in them a feeling of separatism when the school should be the training ground for habits of community, or they will have religious instruction in a faith which is not that of their parents. As a result, the public school system of Champaign actively furthers inculcation in the religious tenets of some faiths, and in the process sharpens the consciousness of religious differences at least among some of the children committed to its care. These are consequences not amenable to statistics. But they are precisely the consequences against which the Constitution was directed when it prohibited the Government common to all from becoming embroiled, however innocently, in the destructive religious conflicts of which the history of even this country records some dark pages.

Mention should not be omitted that the integration of religious instruction within the school system as practiced in Champaign is supported by arguments drawn from educational theories as diverse as those derived from Catholic conceptions and from the writings of John Dewey. Movements like "released time" are seldom single in origin or aim. Nor can the intrusion of religious instruction into the public school system of Champaign be minimized by saying that it absorbs less than an hour a week; in fact, that affords evidence of a design constitutionally objectionable. If it were merely a question of enabling a child to obtain religious instruction with a receptive mind, the thirty or forty-five minutes could readily be found on Saturday or Sunday. If that were all, Champaign might have drawn upon the French system, known in its American manifestation as "dismissed time," whereby one school day is shortened to allow all children to go where they please, leaving those who so desire to go to a religious school. The momentum of the whole school atmosphere and school planning is presumably put behind religious instruction, as given in Champaign, precisely in order to secure for the religious instruction such momentum and planning. To speak of "released time" as being only half or three quarters of an hour is to draw a thread from the fabric.

The foregoing material, hinting that this case is not to be construed as passing on all varieties of released time programs, is reinforced by the following:

We do not consider, as indeed we could not, school programs not before us which, though colloquially characterized as "released time," present situations differing in aspects that may well be constitutionally crucial. Different forms which "released time" has taken during more than thirty years of growth includes programs which, like that before us, could not withstand the test of the Constitution; others may be found unexceptionable. We do not attempt to weigh in the Constitutional scale every separate detail or various combinations of factors which may establish a valid "released time" program.

Returning to the specific case before the Court, the opinion concludes:

We find that the basic Constitutional principle of absolute Separation was violated when the State of Illinois, speaking through its Supreme Court, sustained the school authorities of Champaign in sponsoring and effectively furthering religious beliefs by its educational arrangement.

Separation means separation, not something less. Jefferson's metaphor in describing the relation between Church and State speaks of a "wall of separation," not of a fine line easily overstepped. The public school is at once the symbol of our democracy and the most pervasive means for promoting our common destiny. In no activity of the State is it more vital to keep our divisive forces than in its schools, to avoid confusing, not to say fusing, what the Constitution sought to keep strictly apart. "The great American principle of eternal separation"—Elihu Root's phrase bears repetition—is one of the vital reliances of our Constitutional system for assuring unities among our people stronger than our diversities. It is the Court's duty to enforce this principle in its full integrity.

We renew our conviction that "we have staked the very existence of our country on the faith that complete separation between the state and religion is best for the state and best for religion." *Everson v. Board of Education.* If no where else, in the relation between Church and State, "good fences make good neighbors."

OPINION OF JUSTICE JACKSON

Justice Jackson, who concurred in the decision reached by the Court and joined in the opinion written by Justice Frankfurter, also wrote a separate opinion. He began by expressing doubts about the propriety of the Supreme Court having accepted jurisdiction in this case. He expressed further misgivings about the breadth of the decision rendered, explaining his viewpoint in the following language:

If, however, jurisdiction is found to exist, it is important that we circumscribe our decision with some care. What is asked is not a defensive use of judicial power to set aside a tax levy or reverse a conviction, or to enjoin threats of prosecution or taxation. The relief demanded in this case is the extraordinary writ of mandamus to tell the local Board of Education what it must do. . . . The plaintiff, as she has every right to be, is an avowed atheist. What she has asked of the courts is that they not only end the "released time" plan but also ban every form of teaching which suggests or recognizes that there is a God. She would ban all teaching of the Scriptures. She especially mentions as an example of invasion of her rights "having pupils learn and recite such statements as, 'The Lord is my Shepherd, I shall not want,' " and she objects to teaching that the King James version of the Bible "is called the Christian's Guide Book, the Holy Writ, and the Word of God," and many other similar matters. This Court is directing the Illinois courts generally to sustain plaintiff's complaint without exception of any of these grounds of complaint, without discriminating between them and without laying down any standards to define the limits of the effect of our decision.

To me, the sweep and detail of these complaints is a danger signal which warns of the kind of local controversy we will be required to arbitrate if we do not place appropriate limitation on our decision and exact strict compliance with jurisdictional requirements. . . .

While we may and should end such formal and explicit instruction as the Champaign plan and can at all times prohibit teaching of creed and catechism and ceremonial and can forbid forthright proselyting in the schools, I think it remains to be demonstrated whether it is possible, even if desirable, to comply with such demands as plaintiff's completely to isolate and cast out of secular education all that some people may reasonably regard as religious instruction. Perhaps subjects such as mathematics, physics or chemistry are, or can be, completely secularized. But it would not seem practical to teach either practice or appreciation of the arts if we are to forbid exposure of youth to any religious influences. Music without sacred music, architecture minus the cathedral, or painting without the scriptural themes would be eccentric and incomplete, even from a secular point of view. . . . The fact is that, for good or for ill, nearly everything in our culture worth transmitting, everything which gives meaning to life, is saturated with religious influences, derived from paganism, Judaism, Christianity—both Catholic and Protestant—and other faiths accepted by a large part of the world's peoples. One can hardly respect a system of education that would leave the student wholly ignorant of the currents of religious thought that move world society for a part in which he is being prepared.

The opinions in this case show that the public educational authorities have evolved a considerable variety of practices in dealing with the religious problem. Neighborhoods differ in racial, religious and cultural compositions. It must be expected that they will adopt different customs which will give emphasis to different values and will induce different experiments. And it must be expected that, no matter what practice prevails, there will be many discontented and possibly belligerent minorities. We must leave some flexibility to meet local conditions, some chance to progress by trial and error. While I agree that the religious classes involved here go beyond permissible limits, I also think the complaint demands more than plaintiff is entitled to have granted. . . .

The task of separating the secular from the religious in education is one of magnitude, intricacy and delicacy. To lay down a sweeping constitutional doctrine as demanded by complainant and apparently approved by the Court, applicable alike to all school boards in the nation, "to immediately adopt and enforce rules and regulations prohibiting all instruction in and teaching of religious education in all public schools," is to decree a uniform, rigid and, if we are consistent, an unchanging standard for countless school boards representing and serving highly localized groups which not only differ from each other but which themselves from time to time change attitudes. It seems to me that to do so is to allow zeal for our own ideas of what is good in public instruction to induce us to accept the role of a super board of education for every school district in the nation.

DISSENT

Justice Reed, alone, dissented. Referring to the Court's decision, he said:

. . . As I am convinced that this interpretation of the First Amendment is erroneous, I feel impelled to express the reasons for my disagreement. By directing attention to the many instances of close association of church and state in American society and by recalling that many of these relations are so much part of our tradition and culture that they are accepted without more, this dissent may help in an appraisal of the meaning of the clause of the First Amendment concerning the establishment of religion and of the reasons which lead to the approval or disapproval of the judgment below.

Justice Reed continued by expressing concern about the future impact of the reasoning employed by the principal and concurring opinions:

The reasons for the reversal of the Illinois judgment as they appear in the respective opinions may be summarized by the following excerpts. The opinion of the Court, after stating the facts says: "The foregoing facts without reference to others that appear in the record, show the use of tax-supported property for religious instruction and the close cooperation between the school authorities and the religious council in promoting religious education. . . . And it falls squarely under the ban of the First Amendment (made applicable to the States by the Fourteenth) as we interpreted it in *Everson v. Board of Education.*" Another opinion phrases it thus: "We do not attempt to weigh in the Constitutional scale every separate detail or various combination of factors which may establish a valid 'released time' program. We find that the basic Constitutional principle of absolute separation was violated when the State of Illinois, speaking through its Supreme Court, sustained the school authorities of Champaign in sponsoring and effectively furthering religious beliefs by its educational arrangement." These expressions in the decisions seem to leave open for further litigation variations from the Champaign plan. Actually, however, future cases must run the gauntlet not only of the judgment entered but of the accompanying words of the opinions. I find it difficult to extract from the opinions any conclusion as to what it is in the Champaign plan that is unconstitutional. Is it the use of the school buildings for religious instruction; the release of pupils by the schools for religious instruction during school hours; the so-called assistance by teachers in handing out the request cards to pupils, in keeping lists of them for release and records of their attendance; or the action of the principals in arranging an opportunity for the classes and the appearance of the Council's instructors? None of the reversing opinions say whether the purpose of the Champaign plan for religious instruction during school hours is unconstitutional or whether it is some ingredient used in or omitted from the formula that makes the plan unconstitutional.

From the tenor of the opinions I conclude that their teachings are that any use of a pupil's school time, whether that use is on or off the school grounds, with the necessary school regulations to facilitate attendance, falls under the ban. I reach this conclusion notwithstanding one sentence of indefinite meaning in the second opinion: "We do not consider, as indeed we could not, school programs not before us which, though colloquially characterized as 'released time,' present situations differing in aspects that may well be constitutionally crucial." The use of the words "cooperation," "fusion," "complete hands-off," "integrate" and "integrated" to describe the relations between the school and the Council in the plan evidences this. So does the interpretation of the word "aid." . . . From the holding and the language of the opinions, I can only deduce that religious instruction of public school children during school hours is prohibited. The history of American education is against such an interpretation of the First Amendment.

The opinions do not say in words that the condemned practice of religious education is a law respecting an establishment of religion contrary to the First Amendment. The practice is accepted as a state law by all. I take it that when the opinion of the Court says that "The operation of the state's compulsory education system thus assists and is integrated with the program of religious instruction carried on by separate religious sects" and concludes "That is beyond all question a utilization of the tax-established and tax-supported public school system to aid religious groups to spread their faith," the intention of its author is to rule that this practice is a law "respecting an establishment of religion." This was the basis of *Everson v. Board of Education.* It seems obvious that the action of the School Board in permitting religious education in certain grades of the schools by all faiths did not prohibit the free exercise of religion. As no issue of prohibition upon the free exercise of religion is before us, we need only examine the School Board's action to see if it constitutes an establishment of religion.

The following findings of the Illinois trial court are cited in a footnote to Justice Reed's opinion in order to clarify the facts involved in the case at issue:

The superintendent testified that Jehovah's Witnesses or any other sect would be allowed to teach provided their teachers had proper educational qualifications, so that bad grammar, for instance, would not be taught to the pupils. . . .

Before any faith or other group may obtain permission from the defendant for the similar, free and equal use of rooms in the public school buildings said faith or group must make application to the superintendent of schools . . . who in turn will determine whether or not it is practical for said group to teach in said school system.

The court feels from all the facts in the record that an honest attempt has been made and is being made to permit religious instruction to be given by qualified outside teachers of any sect to people of their own faith in the manner above outlined. The evidence shows that no sect or religious group has ever been denied the right to use the schools in this manner.

The curriculum of studies in the Protestant classes is determined by a committee of the Protestant members of the council of religious education after consultation with representatives of all the different faiths included in said council. The Jewish classes of course would deny the divinity of Jesus Christ. The teaching in the

Catholic classes of course explains to Catholic pupils the teaching of the Catholic religion, and are not shared by other students who are Protestants or Jews. The teachings in the Protestant classes would undoubtedly, from the evidence, teach some doctrines that would not be accepted by the other two religions.

. . . The testimony of the religious education teachers, the secular teachers who testified, and the many children, mostly from Protestant families, who either took or did not take religious education courses, is to the effect that religious education classes have fostered tolerance rather than intolerance.

The Supreme Court of Illinois is quoted:

The religious education courses do not go to the extent of being worship services and do not include prayers or the singing of hymns.

The dissenting opinion goes on to say:

The facts, as stated in the reversing opinions, are adequately set out if we interpret the abstract words used in the light of the concrete incidents of the record.

Serious objection is made to the interpretation given by the Court to the words of the Establishment Clause of the First Amendment which Justice Reed says is not consistent with the history of the Amendment or with the meaning previously given it by the Court:

The phrase "an establishment of religion" may have been intended by Congress to be aimed only at a state church. When the First Amendment was pending in Congress in substantially its present form, "Mr. Madison said, he apprehended the meaning of the words to be, that Congress should not establish a religion, and enforce the legal observation of it by law, nor compel men to worship God in any manner contrary to their conscience." Passing years, however, have brought about acceptance of a broader meaning, although never until today, I believe, has this Court widened its interpretation to any such degree as holding that recognition of the interest of our nation in religion, through the granting, to qualified representatives of the principal faiths, of opportunity to present religion as an optional, extracurricular subject during released school time in public school buildings, was equivalent to the establishment of a religion. . . .

After discussing the views of Jefferson, Justice Reed says:

Thus, the "wall of separation between church and State" that Mr. Jefferson built at the University which he founded did not exclude religious education from that school. The difference between the generality of his statements on the separation of church and State and the specificity of his conclusions on education are considerable. A rule of law should not be drawn from a figure of speech.

Justice Reed asserts that Madison's views likewise are not an adequate basis for the decision rendered and then continues:

This Court summarized the amendment's accepted reach into the religious field, as I understand its scope, in *Everson v. Board of Education.* The Court's opinion quotes the gist of the Court's reasoning in *Everson.* I agree, as there stated, that none of our governmental entities can "set up a church." I agree that they cannot "aid" all or any religions or prefer one "over another." But "aid" must be understood as a purposeful assistance directly to the church itself or to some religious group or organization doing religious work of such a character that it may fairly be said to be performing ecclesiastical functions. "Prefer" must give an advantage to one "over another." I agree that pupils cannot "be released in part from their legal duty" of school attendance upon condition that they attend religious classes. But as Illinois has held that it is within the discretion of the School Board to permit absence from school for religious instruction no legal duty of school attendance is violated. . . . If the sentence in the Court's opinion, concerning the pupils' release from legal duty, is intended to mean that the Constitution forbids a school to excuse a pupil from secular control during school hours to attend voluntarily a class in religious education, whether in or out of school buildings, I disagree. Of course, no tax can be levied to support organizations intended "to teach or practice religion." I agree too that the state cannot influence one toward religion against his will or punish him for his beliefs. Champaign's religious education course does none of these things.

It seems clear to me that the "aid" referred to by the Court in the *Everson* case could not have been those incidental advantages that religious bodies, with other groups similarly situated, obtain as a by-product of organized society. This explains the well-known fact that all churches receive "aid" from government in the form of freedom from taxation. The *Everson* decision itself justified the transportation of children to church schools by New Jersey for safety reasons. It accords with *Cochran v. Louisiana State Board of Education*, where this Court upheld a free textbook statute of Louisiana against a charge that it aided private schools on the ground that the books were for the education of the children, not to aid religious schools. . . .

Well-recognized and long-established practices support the validity of the Illinois statute here in question. That statute, as construed in this case, is comparable to those in many states. All differ to some extent. New York may be taken as a fair example.

At this point the New York practice and the statutory basis for that practice are discussed in a lengthy footnote which is omitted here because the New York practices are more relevant in connection with the *Zorach* case which is found later in this chapter.

The dissenting opinion continues:

In many states the program is under the supervision of a religious council composed of delegates who are themselves communicants of various faiths. . . . In some, instruction is given outside the school buildings; in others, within these buildings. Metropolitan centers like New York usually would have available quarters convenient to the schools. Unless smaller cities and rural communities use the school building at times that do not interfere with recitations, they may be compelled to give up religious education. I understand that pupils not taking religious education usually are given other work of a secular nature within the schools. Since all these states use the facilities of the schools to aid the religious education to some extent, their desire to permit religious education to school children is thwarted by this Court's judgment. Under it, as I understand its language, children cannot be released or dismissed from school to attend classes in religion while other children must remain to pursue secular education. Teachers cannot keep the records as to which pupils are to be dismissed and which retained. To do so is said to be an "aid" in establishing religion; the use of public money for religion.

At this point some of the decisions of the various state courts are mentioned in a footnote:

Many uses of religious material in the public schools in a manner that has some religious significance have been sanctioned by state courts. These practices have been permitted: reading selections from the King James Bible without comment; reading the Bible and repeating the Lord's Prayer; teaching the Ten Commandments; saying prayers; and using textbooks based upon the Bible and emphasizing its fundamental teachings. When conducted in a sectarian manner reading from the Bible and singing hymns in the school's morning exercise has been prohibited as has using the Bible as a textbook. . . . It has been held to be constitutional for the school authorities to prohibit the reading of the Bible in the public schools. There is a conflict of authority on the constitutionality of the use of public school buildings for religious services held outside of school hours. The constitutionality, under state constitutions, of furnishing free textbooks and free transportation to parochial school children is in conflict.

Justice Reed points out that there are many examples of federal practices in relation to religion that appear to be relevant.

The dissenting opinion concludes by saying:

With the general statements in the opinions concerning the constitutional requirements that the nation and the states, by virtue of the First and Fourteenth Amendments, may "make no law respecting an establishment of religion"; I am in agreement. But, in the light of the meaning given to those words by the precedents, customs, and practices which I have detailed above, I cannot agree with the Court's conclusion that when pupils compelled by law to go to school for secular education are released from school so as to attend the religious classes, churches are unconstitutionally aided. . . . The prohibition of enactments respecting the establishment of religion do not bar every friendly gesture between church and state. It is not an absolute prohibition against every conceivable situation where the two may work together, any more than the other provisions of the First Amendment—free speech, free press—are absolutes. If abuses occur, such as the use of the instruction hour for sectarian purposes, I have no doubt, . . . that Illinois will promptly correct them. If they are of a kind that tend to the establishment of a church or interfere with the free exercise of religion, this Court is open for a review of any erroneous decision. This Court cannot be too cautious in upsetting practices embedded in our society by many years of experience. A state is entitled to have great leeway in its legislation when dealing with the important social problems of its population. A definite violation of legislative limits must be established. The Constitution should not be stretched to forbid national customs in the way courts act to reach arrangements to avoid federal taxation. Devotion to the great principle of religious liberty should not lead us into a rigid interpretation of the constitutional guarantee that conflicts with accepted habits of our people. This is an instance where, for me, the history of past practices is determinative of the meaning of a constitutional clause, not a decorous introduction to the study of its text. The judgment should be affirmed.

In this case it was decided that releasing public school pupils during school hours to receive religious instruction in public school classrooms violated the Establishment Clause of the First Amendment.

The sharp difference of viewpoint between the dissenting opinion written by Justice Reed and the Court's opinion was reflected in the public reaction to the ruling in the McCollum case. On the one hand, the Court's ruling was called a strong reassertion of constitutional protection from an intermingling of church and state. On the other hand, the view was expressed that a blow had been struck against religious liberty by a perversion of the meaning of the language of the First Amendment. Typical of some of the extreme arguments expressed by proponents of the latter view was the following language used by William David Stout in the March, 1949, issue of the *Kentucky Law Journal*:

In the light of what has been said, the following conclusions appear to be self-evident: First, the First Amendment means traditionally that Congress cannot establish a church; second, this is due more to the sectarian character of American religion than to any real desire to completely isolate government from the basic moral concepts that we traditionally speak of as Christians; and third, even if it were possible to completely separate religious concepts from politics by legislation, it would have to be done at the expense of society's right to pass its ideals down through successive generations. American traditions can no more be separated from religious concepts than can those of the Middle Ages without the disruption of the whole social and political structure. The Supreme Court, through its decision in the McCallon [sic] case, has opened a virtual Pandora's box, the results of which are still in doubt. It has also brought home the fact that the First Amendment as stated is not sufficiently clear to meet modern situations, and as traditionally interpreted either becomes an empty phrase or, if stretched to the limit, an outright threat to our basic traditions. It seems that before we can properly interpret our constitutional guarantees against religious establishment, indeed before we can feel legally secure in using our society's chief attitude moulding agency for bringing up our children in the true concepts of our society, we may need to pass a new amendment either to clarify or replace the wording of the First Amendment.

Calmer voices pointed out that the application of the rule stated by the Court was quite narrow and that there was little likelihood that all "released time" instruction for public school children would be banned by the Court in future rulings.

Not long after the ruling in the *McCollum* case, suit was brought in New York to test the assumption just stated. It was sought to have the Courts rule that the released-time procedure

used in that state was contrary to the constitutional requirements of the First and Fourteenth Amendments under the authority of *McCollum*.

Under the New York plan the children were dismissed
from their public school classes during school hours to attend
sectarian religious instruction away from the public school. The
issue to be determined was whether or not such a procedure
would violate the Establishment Clause of the First Amendment.

This case, *Zorach* v. *Clauson*, reached the New York
Court of Appeals (the highest appellate court in that state) in
1951. In June of that year a decision was rendered sustaining the
constitutionality of the New York procedures. The Court stated
in part:

It is thus clear beyond cavil that the Constitution does not
demand that every friendly gesture between church and State shall
be discountenanced.

The "wall of separation," the Court of Appeals said,
should be "a reasonable line between friends" rather than "an
iron curtain between foes."

The majority further pointed out that the *McCollum*
decision was by its own words limited to the particular and
peculiar facts involved in that case.

The dissenting opinion voiced the view that there was
no valid distinction between the facts of the *McCollum* case and
the case at bar. This opinion also used the following language:

It may well be that there are children growing up untutored in
matters religious and, if that be so, it is a matter for grave concern.
Considerations of fundamental principles, however, are involved
when an attempt is made to enable religious groups to cure that
lack through the instrumentality of the public school.

The plaintiff then appealed to the United States Supreme
Court and the decision rendered in that case will be excerpted
and commented upon in the remainder of this chapter.

ZORACH et al. v. CLAUSON et al. CONSTITUTING THE BOARD OF EDUCATION OF THE CITY OF NEW YORK et al.[2]

The opinion of the Court, delivered by Justice Douglas, was agreed to by six Justices (Vinson, Reed, Burton, Clark, Minton, and, of course, Douglas). Three Justices (Black, Frankfurter, and Jackson) dissented.

The following description of the New York City program is adapted from the information found in footnotes to Justice Reed's dissenting opinion in the *McCollum* case and to the Court's opinion in the Zorach case.

The New York State law provided that:

1. A minor required by the provisions of part one of this article to attend upon instruction shall attend regularly as prescribed where he resides or is employed, for the entire time the appropriate public school or classes are in session. . . .
2. Absence for religious observance and education shall be permitted under rules that the commissioner shall establish.

Acting under the authority of this law the New York State Commissioner of Education issued the following regulations:

1. Absence of a pupil from school during school hours for religious observance and education to be had outside the school building and grounds will be excused upon the request in writing signed by the parent or guardian of the pupil.
2. The courses in religious observance and education must be maintained and operated by and under the control of a duly constituted religious body or of duly constituted religious bodies.

[2] 343 U.S. 306. Decided April 28, 1952.

3. Pupils must be registered for the courses and a copy of the registration filed with the local public school authorities.

4. Reports of attendance of pupils upon such courses shall be filed with the principal or teacher at the end of each week.

5. Such absence shall be for not more than one hour each week at the close of a session at a time to be fixed by the local school authorities.

6. In the event that more than one school for religious observance and education is maintained in any district, the hour for absence for each particular public school in such district shall be the same for all such religious schools.

New York City regulations adopted by the Board of Education provide that:

1. No announcement of any kind will be made in the public schools relative to the program.

2. The religious organizations and parents will assume full responsibility for attendance at the religious schools and will explain any failures to attend on the weekly attendance reports.

3. Classes in religious education are to be held outside of school buildings.

4. Establishment of the program rests in the initiative of the church and home.

5. Enrollment is voluntary and accomplished by this technique: the church distributes cards to the parents and these are filled out and presented to the school.

6. Records of enrollment and arrangements for release are handled by school authorities.

7. Discipline is the responsibility of the church.

8. Children who do not attend are kept at school and given other work.

9. Students who are released will be dismissed from school in the usual way.

10. There shall be no comment by any principal or teacher on

attendance or nonattendance of any pupil upon religious instruction.

Justice Douglas' opinion opened with a summary of the situation at issue:

New York City has a program which permits its public schools to release students during the school day so that they may leave the school buildings and school grounds and go to religious centers for religious instruction or devotional exercises. A student is released on written request of his parents. Those not released stay in the classrooms. The churches make weekly reports to the schools, sending a list of children who have been released from public school but who have not reported for religious instruction.

The case at issue is distinguished from the *McCollum* case:

This "released time" program involves neither religious instruction in public school classrooms nor the expenditure of public funds. All costs, including the application blanks, are paid by the religious organizations. The case is therefore unlike *McCollum* v. *Board of Education*, which involved a "released time" program from Illinois. In that case the classrooms were turned over to religious instructors. We accordingly held that the program violated the First Amendment which (by reason of the Fourteenth Amendment) prohibits the states from establishing religion or prohibiting its free exercise.

The arguments of the plaintiffs are summarized as follows:

Appellants, who are taxpayers and residents of New York City and whose children attend its public schools, challenge the present law, contending it is in essence not different from the one involved in the *McCollum* case. Their argument, stated elaborately in various ways, reduces itself to this: the weight and influence of the school is put behind a program for religious instruction; public school teachers police it, keeping tab on students who are released; the classroom activities come to a halt while the students released for religious instruction are on leave; the school is a crutch on which the churches are leaning for support in their religious training; without the cooperation of the schools this "released time" program, like the one in the *McCollum* case, would be futile and ineffective.

Justice Douglas points out that the educational merits of the "released-time" program are not involved:

The briefs and arguments are replete with data bearing on the merits of this type of "released time" program. Views *pro* and *con* are expressed, based on practical experience with these programs and with their implications. We do not stop to summarize these materials nor to burden the opinion with an analysis of them. For they involve considerations not germane to the narrow constitutional issue presented. They largely concern the wisdom of the system, its efficiency from an educational point of view, and the political considerations which have motivated its adoption or rejection in some communities. Those matters are of no concern here, since our problem reduces itself to whether New York by this system has either prohibited the "free exercise" of religion or has made a law "respecting an establishment of religion" within the meaning of the First Amendment.

The Court rejects the idea that the "released-time" plan in question is in violation of the "Free Exercise" clause of the First Amendment:

It takes obtuse reasoning to inject any issue of the "free exercise" of religion into the present case. No one is forced to go to the religious classroom and no religious exercise or instruction is brought to the classrooms of the public schools. A student need not take religious instruction. He is left to his own desires as to the manner or time of his religious devotions, if any.

There is a suggestion that the system involves the use of coercion to get public school students into religious classrooms. There is no evidence in the record before us that supports this conclusion.

The contention that a violation of the Establishment Clause occurred is also rejected:

Moreover, apart from that claim of coercion, we do not see how New York by this type of "released time" program has made a law respecting an establishment of religion within the meaning of the First Amendment. . . . There cannot be the slightest doubt that the First Amendment reflects the philosophy that Church and State should be separated. And so far as interference with the "free exercise" of religion and an "establishment" of religion are concerned, the separation must be complete and unequivocal. The First Amendment within the scope of its coverage permits no exception; the prohibition is absolute.

The true meaning and purpose of the First Amendment is discussed:

The First Amendment, however, does not say that in every and all respects there should be a separation of Church and State. Rather, it studiously defines the manner, the specific ways, in which there shall be no concert or union or dependency one on the other. That is the common sense of the matter. Otherwise the state and religion would be aliens to each other—hostile, suspicious, and even unfriendly. . . .

. . . The nullification of this law would have wide and profound effects. A Catholic student applies to his teacher for permission to leave the school during hours on a Holy Day of Obligation to attend a mass. A Jewish student asks his teacher for permission to be excused for Yom Kippur. A Protestant wants the afternoon off for a family baptismal service. In each case the teacher requires parental consent in writing. In each case the teacher, in order to make sure the student is not a truant, goes further and requires a report from the priest, the rabbi, or the minister. The teacher in other words cooperates in a religious program to the extent of making it possible for her students to participate in it. Whether she does it occasionally for a few students, regularly for one, or pursuant to a systematized program designed to further the religious needs of all the students does not alter the character of the act.

We are a religious people whose institutions presuppose a Supreme Being. We guarantee the freedom to worship as one chooses. We make room for as wide a variety of beliefs and creeds as the spiritual needs of man deem necessary. . . . But we find no constitutional requirement which makes it necessary for government to be hostile to religion and to throw its weight against efforts to widen the effective scope of religious influence. . . .

In concluding, the opinion restresses the distinction between the *McCollum* case and the present one:

In the *McCollum* case the classrooms were used for religious instruction and the force of the public school was used to promote that instruction. Here, as we have said, the public schools do no more than accommodate their schedules to a program of outside religious instruction. We follow the *McCollum* case. But we cannot expand it to cover the present released time program unless separation of Church and State means that public institutions can make no adjustments of their schedules to accommodate the religious needs of the people. We cannot read into the Bill of Rights such a philosophy of hostility to religion.

DISSENT

Justice Black, dissenting, left no doubt about his position that the present case was not distinguishable from the *McCollum* case. He said:

Illinois ex rel. McCollum v. *Board of Education* held invalid as an "establishment of religion" an Illinois system under which school children, compelled by law to go to public schools, were freed from some hours of required school work on condition that they attend special religious classes held in the school buildings. Although the classes were taught by sectarian teachers neither employed nor paid by the state, the state did use its power to further the program by releasing some of the children from regular classwork, insisting that those released attend the religious classes, and requiring that those who remained behind do some kind of academic work while the others received their religious training. We said this about the Illinois system:

> Pupils compelled by law to go to school for secular education are released in part from their legal duty upon the condition that they attend the religious classes. This is beyond all

question a utilization of the tax-established and tax-supported public school system to aid religious groups to spread their faith. And it falls squarely under the ban of the First Amendment . . .

I see no difference between the invalid Illinois system and that of New York here sustained. Except for the use of the school buildings in Illinois, there is no difference between the systems which I consider even worthy of mention. In the New York program, as in that of Illinois, the school authorities release some of the children on the condition that they attend the religious classes, get reports on whether they attend, and hold the other children in the school building until the religious hour is over. As we attempted to make categorically clear, the *McCollum* decision would have been the same if the religious classes had not been held in the school buildings. . . . *McCollum* thus held that Illinois could not constitutionally manipulate the compelled classroom hours of its compulsory school machinery so as to channel children into sectarian classes. Yet that is exactly what the Court holds New York can do.

Comment is made on the furor stirred up by the *McCollum* decision:

I am aware that our *McCollum* decision on separation of Church and State has been subjected to a most searching examination throughout the country. Probably few opinions from this Court in recent years have attracted more attention or stirred wider debate. Our insistence on a "wall between Church and State which must be kept high and impregnable" has seemed to some a correct exposition of the philosophy and a true interpretation of the language of the First Amendment to which we should strictly adhere. With equal conviction and sincerity, others have thought the *McCollum* decision fundamentally wrong and have pledged continuous warfare against it.

The opinion concludes:

In dissenting today I mean to give more than routine approval to our *McCollum* decision. I mean also to reaffirm my faith in the fundamental philosophy expressed in *McCollum* and *Everson* v. *Board of Education*. That reaffirmance can be brief because of the exhaustive opinions in those recent cases.

. . . Here the sole question is whether New York can use its compulsory education laws to help religious sects get attendants presumably too unenthusiastic to go unless moved to do so by the pressure of this state machinery. That this is the plan, purpose, design and consequence of the New York program cannot be denied. The State thus makes religious sects beneficiaries of its power to compel children to attend secular schools. Any use of such coercive power by the state to help or to hinder some religious sects or to prefer all religious sects over non-believers or vice versa is just what I think the First Amendment forbids. In considering whether a state has entered this forbidden field the question is not whether it has entered too far but whether it has entered at all. New York is manipulating its compulsory education laws to help religious sects get pupils. This is not separation but combination of Church and State.

Under our system of religious freedom, people have gone to their religious sanctuaries not because they feared the law but because they loved their God. The choice of all has been as free as the choice of those who answered the call to worship moved only by the music of the old Sunday morning church bells. The spiritual mind of man has thus been free to believe, disbelieve, or doubt, without repression, great or small, by the heavy hand of government. Statutes authorizing such repression have been stricken. . . . The First Amendment has lost much if the religious follower and the atheist are no longer to be judicially regarded as entitled to equal justice under law.

State help to religion injects political and party prejudices into a holy field. It too often substitutes force for prayer, hate for love, and persecution for persuasion. Government should not be allowed, under cover of the soft euphemism of "co-operation," to steal into the sacred area of religious choice.

ANOTHER DISSENTING OPINION

Justice Frankfurter expressed his agreement with the dissent delivered by Justice Jackson but, in addition, filed a separate opinion in which he expressed himself in these words:

The Court tells us that in the maintenance of its public schools "The State government can close its doors or suspend its operations" so that its citizens may be free for religious devotions or instruction. If that were the issue, it would not rise to the dignity of a constitutional controversy. Of course, a State may provide that the classes in its schools shall be dismissed, for any reason, or no reason, on fixed days, or for special occasions. The essence of this case is that the school system did not "close its doors" and did not "suspend its operations." There is all the difference in the world between letting the children out of school and letting some of them out of school into religious classes. If everyone is free to make what use he will of time wholly unconnected from schooling required by law—those who wish sectarian instruction devoting it to that purpose, those who have ethical instruction at home, to that, those who study music, to that—then of course there is no conflict with the Fourteenth Amendment.

The pith of the case is that formalized religious instruction is substituted for other school activity which those who do not participate in the released time program are compelled to attend. The school system is very much in operation during this kind of released time. If its doors are closed, they are closed upon those students who do not attend the religious instruction, in order to keep them within the school. That is the very thing which raises the constitutional issue. It is not met by disregarding it. Failure to discuss this issue does not take it out of the case.

The opinion is highly critical of the view that there was no coercion involved here and deplores the fact that evidence offered on this issue had not been admitted.

Justice Frankfurter then reaffirms his belief in the correctness of the *McCollum* decision in the final paragraphs of his dissent:

The result in the *McCollum* case . . . was based on principles that received unanimous acceptance by this Court barring only a single vote. I agree with Mr. Justice Black that those principles are disregarded in reaching the result in this case. Happily they are not disavowed by the Court. From this I draw the hope that in the future variations of the problem which are bound to come here, these principles may again be honored in the observance.

FURTHER DISSENT

Justice Jackson in an opinion which at some points can only be described as bitter, expressed the following views in his dissenting opinion which is given in full:

This released time program is founded upon a use of the State's power of coercion, which, for me, determines its unconstitutionality. Stripped to its essentials, the plan has two stages: first, that the State compel each student to yield a large part of his time for public secular education; and second, that some of it be "released" to him on condition that he devote it to sectarian religious purposes.

No one suggests that the Constitution would permit the State directly to require this "released" time to be spent "under the control of a duly constituted religious body." This program accomplishes that forbidden result by indirection. If public education were taking so much of the pupils' time as to injure the public or the students' welfare by encroaching upon their religious opportunity, simply shortening everyone's school day would facilitate voluntary and optional attendance at Church classes. But that suggestion is rejected upon the ground that if they are free many students will not go to the Church. Hence, they must be deprived of freedom for this period, with Church attendance put to them as one of the two permissible ways of using it.

The greater effectiveness of this system over voluntary attendance after school hours is due to the truant officer who, if the youngster fails to go to the Church school, dogs him back to the public schoolroom. Here schooling is more or less suspended during the "released time" so the nonreligious attendants will not forge ahead of the churchgoing absentees. But it serves as a temporary jail for a pupil who will not go to Church. It takes more subtlety of mind than I possess to deny that this is governmental constraint in support of religion. It is as unconstitutional, in my view, when exerted by indirection as when exercised forthrightly.

As one whose children, as a matter of free choice, have been sent to privately supported Church schools, I may challenge the Court's suggestion that opposition to this plan can only be antireligious, atheistic, or agnostic. My evangelistic brethren confuse an objection to compulsion with an objection to religion. It is possible to hold a faith with enough confidence to believe that what should be rendered to God does not need to be decided and collected by Caesar.

The day that this country ceases to be free for irreligion it will cease to be free for religion—except for the sect that can win political power. The same epithetical jurisprudence used by the Court today to beat down those who oppose pressuring children into some religion can devise as good epithets tomorrow against those who object to pressuring them into a favored religion. And, after all, if we concede to the State power and wisdom to single out "duly constituted religious" bodies as exclusive alternatives for compulsory secular instruction, it would be logical to also uphold the power and wisdom to choose the true faith among those "duly constituted." We start down a rough road when we begin to mix compulsory public education with compulsory godliness.

A number of Justices just short of a majority of the majority that promulgates today's passionate dialectics joined answering them in *Illinois ex rel. McCollum v. Board of Education.* The distinction attempted between that case and this is trivial, almost to the point of cynicism, magnifying its nonessential details and disparaging compulsion which was the underlying reason for invalidity. A reading of the Court's opinion in that case along with its opinion in this case will show such difference of overtones and undertones as to make clear that the *McCollum* case has passed like a storm in a teacup. The wall which the Court was professing to erect between Church and State has become even more warped and twisted than I expected. Today's judgment will be more interesting to students of psychology and of the judicial processes than to students of constitutional law.

THE MEANING OF THE *McCOLLUM* AND *ZORACH* CASES

The general language used in the two cases included in this chapter should not be construed so as to change the fact that only two matters were decided:

1. A plan for "released time" which involves the use of public school classrooms is clearly held to be a contravention of the requirements of the First Amendment to the Constitution. On this point there was near unanimity.

2. The New York plan whereby children are released from the public schools for religious instruction elsewhere was held unobjectionable insofar as constitutional requirements were concerned. While the majority (6–3) agreed on this viewpoint there was a very forceful protest expressed by the dissenting Justices.

There are, of course, many other "released time" plans. The constitutionality of none of these has been decided by these two cases. Yet, the fact is that after over ten years no other case involving the constitutional validity of a "released time" program has reached the Supreme Court. The reason for this appears to be obvious. Any prospective litigant could conclude with a reasonable degree of certainty on the basis of *McCollum* and *Zorach* that very little would be gained from a decision approving or disapproving any other plan from a constitutional standpoint. If a plan were to be declared invalid it would be a relatively simple matter to adjust procedures to bring the case within the *Zorach* rule and thus overcome the adjudicated invalidity. By the same token, no school system would be so foolhardy as to insist on a program similar to that declared constitutionally invalid in the *McCollum* case in the face of any opposition.

It can thus be seen that even though only two actual plans were considered, for all practical purposes the whole issue of the legality of "released time" programs has been effectively determined.

CHAPTER 7

A STATE-COMPOSED PRAYER
IN THE CLASSROOM

ALL THAT HAD come before became prelude when the Supreme Court of the United States accepted jurisdiction in *Engel* v. *Vitale* and agreed to decide whether or not a prayer composed by the New York State Board of Regents could constitutionally be recited in public school classrooms.

When the Supreme Court in June 1962 rendered its decision, the storm of protests and of approval made the reactions to *McCollum* and other previous cases appear very mild indeed. In fact, the public agitation over this decision was much greater than that which followed the much broader decision in the *Schempp* case a year later.

THE FACTS AND ISSUES

The facts involved in *Engel* are very simple: the New York State Board of Regents composed a short prayer worded as follows:

Almighty God, we acknowledge our dependence upon Thee, and we beg Thy blessings upon us, our parents, our teachers and our country.

The Board recommended that this prayer be recited as part of the opening exercises in public school classrooms throughout the state of New York. Most school districts followed this recommendation and required the recital. The question of compulsion was not involved as provisions were made for nonparticipation by those not wishing to take part.

A group of parents who were members of the Jewish faith, of the Society for Ethical Culture, and of the Unitarian Church, as well as one who was a nonbeliever brought suit to bar the recital of this prayer on the grounds that such a recital was contrary to the Establishment Clause of the First Amendment.

Since the facts themselves were not in dispute, no trial was held and the various court decisions which we shall examine were based on the pleadings filed by the parties.

THE TRIAL COURT RULES

The case was first heard by the Supreme Court of Nassau County. (In New York State the "Supreme" Court is a trial court.) Justice Meyer held that there was no valid constitutional objection to the recital of this prayer so long as adequate provisions were made to excuse those who did not wish to participate. In his decision, he first reviewed the history of efforts to compose nonsectarian prayers and then examined the history of prayer in New York State classrooms. He quoted from the 1912 State Department of Education Annual Report, which stated that a series of rulings from 1837 to 1909 had held that the saying of a prayer in the public school classroom was unobjectionable:

. . . teacher might open his school with prayer provided he does not encroach upon the hours allotted to instruction and provided that the attendance of scholars was not exacted as a matter of school discipline.

Justice Meyer pointed out that in 1853 the State Superintendent had ruled that a teacher should not compel Catholic children to join in prayer or read the Bible. He then quoted from a statement by Superintendent Spicer in 1839:

Both parties have rights: the one to bring up their children in the practice of publicly thanking their Creator for His protection and invoking His Blessing; the other of declining in behalf of their children the religious services of any person in whose creed they may not concur or for other reasons satisfactory to themselves. These rights are reciprocal and should be protected equally and neither should interfere with the other. Those who desire that their children should engage in public prayer have no right to compel other children to unite in the exercise, against the wishes of their parents. Nor have those who object to this time, place or manner of praying, or to the person who conducts the exercises a right to deprive the other class of the opportunity of habituating their child to what they conceive an imperious duty.

In denying the demand that the practice of reciting this prayer be banned in the classroom, Justice Meyer states:

It is, however, also contended that the recognition of prayer is an integral part of our national heritage, one that, therefore, the (Establishment) clause cannot have been intended to outlaw the practice in schools any more than for the rest of public life; that is, that prayer in the schools is permissible not as a means of teaching "spiritual values" but because traditionally and particularly at the time of the adoption of the First and Fourteenth Amendments, this was the accepted practice. With this argument, the court agrees. . . .

APPEAL TO THE APPELLATE DIVISION

In October of 1960 four of the judges of the Appellate Division (an intermediate appellate court in New York State's judicial system) affirmed the decision of the lower court. Justice Bedlock concurred in the principle agreed to by his colleagues but dissented on a matter of procedure. He stated that he felt that the prayer in question was not "an act of religious training and teaching."

NEW YORK STATE'S HIGHEST COURT RULES

In July of 1961 a decision was rendered by the Court of Appeal of the State of New York. This is the highest appellate court of the state. Of the seven judges, five voted to affirm the lower courts' decisions and two dissented. The principal majority opinion was written by Chief Judge Desmond who stated in part:

What remains of appellants' argument is this: that the saying of the "Regents prayer" as a daily school exercise is a form of State-sponsored religious education and is accordingly an unconstitutional "establishment of religion." In the utterance of these reverential words was "religious education," then providing such education would be so far beyond the powers of a public school board as to be wholly arbitrary and unlawful, so that the courts would need no constitutional warrant for forbidding it. But it is not "religious education" nor is it the practice of or establishment of religion in any reasonable meaning of those phrases. Saying this simple prayer may be, according to the broadest possible dictionary definition, an act of "religion," but when the Founding Fathers prohibited an "establishment of religion" they were referring to official adoption of, or favor to, one or more sects. They could not have meant to prohibit mere professions of belief in God for, if that were so, they themselves in many ways were violating their rule when and after they adopted it. Not only is this prayer not a violation of the First Amendment (no decision of this or of the United States Supreme Court says or suggests that it is) but a holding that it is such a violation would be in defiance of all American history, and such a holding would destroy a part of the essential foundations of the American governmental structure.

The "Regents prayer" is an acknowledgment of our dependence upon Almighty God and a petition for the bestowal of His blessings. It includes an acknowledgment of the existence of a Supreme Being just as does the Declaration of Independence and the Constitutions of each of the 50 States of the Union, including our own. In construing even a Constitution some attention must be paid to the obvious intent of those who drafted it and adopted it . . . That the First Amendment was ever intended to forbid as an "establishment of religion" a simple declaration of belief in God is so contrary to history as to be impossible of acceptance. No historical fact is so easy to prove by literally countless illustrations as the fact that belief and trust in a Supreme Being was from the beginning and has been continuously part of the very essence of the American plan of government and society. The references to the Deity in the Declaration of Independence; the words of our National Anthem: "In God is our trust"; the motto on our coins; the daily prayers in Congress; the universal practice in official oaths of calling upon God to witness the truth; the official Thanksgiving proclamations beginning with those of the Continental Congress and the First Congress of the United States and continuing till the present; the provisions for chaplaincies in the armed forces; the directions by Congress in modern times for a National Day of Prayer and for the insertion of the words "under God" in the Pledge of Allegiance to the Flag; innumerable solemn utterances by our Presidents and other leaders—all these and many more make historically unescapable the flat statement in *Zorach* v. *Clauson* . . . that "We are a religious people whose institutions presuppose a Supreme Being" . . .

. . . It is an indisputable and historically provable fact that belief and trust in a Creator has always been regarded as an integral and inseparable part of the fabric of our fundamental institutions. It is not a matter of majority power or minority protection. Belief in a Supreme Being is as essential and permanent a feature of the American governmental system as is freedom of worship, equality under the law and due process of law. Like them it is an American absolute, an application of the natural law beliefs on which the Republic was founded and which in turn presuppose an Omnipotent Being.

The motives and purposes of the Regents and of the local board are noble. The success of the practice is problematical. But there is no problem of constitutionality.

CONCURRING OPINIONS

In a concurring opinion Judge Froessel stated in part:

The narrow question presented is: Do the Federal and State Constitutions prohibit the recitation by children in our public schools of the 22 words acknowledging dependence upon Almighty God, and invoking His blessing upon them, their parents and teachers, and upon our country? To say that they do seems to me to stretch the so-called separation of church and State doctrine beyond reason.

History and common experience teach us that the perception of a Supreme Being, commonly called God, is experienced in the lives of most human beings. Some, it is true, escape it, or think they do for a time. In any event, that perception is manifest, independent of any particular religion or church, and has become the foundation of virtually every recognized religious faith—indeed, the common denominator. One may earnestly believe in God, without being attached to any particular religion or church. Hence a rule permitting public school children, willing to do so, to acknowledge their dependence upon Him, and to invoke His blessings, can hardly be called a "law respecting an establishment of religion" or "prohibiting the free exercise thereof" in transgression of the First Amendment, which in nowise prohibits the recognition of God, or laws respecting such recognition.

The challenged recitation follows the pledge of allegiance, which itself refers to God. School children are permitted to sing "America," the fourth stanza of which is indeed a prayer, invoking the protection of "God," "Author of Liberty." The preamble to our State Constitution, which is taught in our public schools, provides: "We the People of the State of New York, grateful to Almighty God for our Freedom." Virtually every State Constitution in the United States, as well as the Declaration of Independence, contains similar references. To say that such references, and others of like nature employed in the executive, legislative and judicial branches of our Government . . . unrelated to any particular religion or church, may be sanctioned by public officials everywhere but in the public school room defies understanding.

The opinion concludes with the following:

As we see it, then, the challenged recitation was rightly upheld. It is not compulsory, is clearly nonsectarian in language, and neither directly nor indirectly even suggests belief in any form of organized or established religion. It permits each child to express gratitude to God and to invoke His blessing, to be steadfast in the faith of his acceptance if he has one; it compels no one, directly or indirectly, to do anything, if that be his or his parents' wish. All remain free, and thus we do not show preference as between "those who believe in no religion" and "those who do believe."

Judge Burke in a second concurring opinion used even stronger terms:

This interpretation rests on a misunderstanding. There is no language in the amendment which gives the slightest basis for the interpolation of a Marxist concept that mandates a prescribed ethic. According to the opinion, the separation of church and State which was intended to encourage *religious* interests among our people would become the constitutional basis for the *compulsory exclusion of any religious element* and the consequent promotion and advancement of atheism. It is not merely neutrality to prevent voluntary prayer to a Creator; it is an interference by the courts, contrary to the plain language of the Constitution, on the side of those who oppose religion.

DISSENTING OPINION

Judge Dye wrote a dissenting opinion in which he stated, after reviewing the facts involved:

No one doubts for a moment that we are a religious people. It can be safely said that under no government—past or present—have the people enjoyed such an untrammeled freedom to worship as they please and to indulge such freedom in more different ways and according to more diverse tenets and beliefs than do the people of the United States. The number of sects and religious groups are almost countless, due, no doubt, to the varied origins of our hetero-

geneous population who have come here seeking, among other
things, an asylum from religious persecution and a freedom to gain
salvation in their own way.

The previous decisions of the Supreme Court of the
United States bearing on this matter are next reviewed, after
which Judge Dye says:

Running through the fabric of these definitive decisions, like the
pattern of a tree of life in an intricate tapestry, is a clearly defined
line of demarcation between church and State, which may not be
overstepped in the slightest degree in favor of either the church or
the State. In such light, a board of education may not require the
saying of the Regents prayer as a daily school procedure. It is a form
of State-sponsored religious education; in fact, according to the
Regents, its purpose is "teaching our children, as set forth in the
Declaration of Independence, that Almighty God is their Creator"
(1951 Statement of Belief) and "will give to the student an understanding and appreciation of his role as an individual endowed by
his Creator . . . and of reverence for Almighty God." It would
thus "fulfill its (the school's) high function of supplementing the
training of the home" (Fundamental Beliefs, Regents Recom-
mendations, adopted March 25, 1955). This requirement falls
squarely within the categories of disability accounting for the decisions in *Everson* and *McCollum* (supra): use of public school
classrooms during regular school hours, limitation of participation
to those children whose parents consent and, in addition, being led
by a teacher or by a person designated by the teacher. Under such
announced purpose and method of performance, it cannot be less
than instruction contrary to the establishment and freedom clauses,
nor can the requirement be excused on the theory that the saying
of the prayer—although conducted in the presence of the student
body in the assembly hall of the classroom—is nonetheless a voluntary act, since no child is "required or encouraged to join in said
prayer against his or his wishes" (Answering Affidavit), or on the
theory that during the saying the child may remain silent, leave the
room or report late. This is no answer, for it contains the very
elements the prayer is supposed to eliminate: divisiveness, a type of

compulsion, exerting as it does a pressure which an immature child is unable to resist because of his inherent desire to conform, and constituting a subtle interference by the State with the religious freedom guaranteed by the First Amendment then . . .

Justice Dye continues:

The mere circumstance that the children of these petitioners may constitute a minority is no justification for rejecting their petition. The guarantees of the Bill of Rights, of which the First Amendment is the very cornerstone, were designed to protect minorities, which include diverse religious sects and atheists. While majority rule is an accepted incident of the political aspects of the democratic process, nothing in the Bill of Rights permits imposing the will of a majority—even in the slightest degree—upon an objecting minority, contrary to its protective cloak . . .

As to the nonsectarian nature of the prayer it is said:

The sponsors of the Regents prayer claim that it is nonsectarian in nature, a simple statement acknowledging the existence of and our dependence upon a Supreme Being; that such reference is of much the same character as the reference to God in various holiday programs (i.e., Christmas, Easter, Thanksgiving Day), in various official oaths, in invocations and benedictions said at most public gatherings, at meetings of some official bodies as well as in the inscription of the motto "In God We Trust" on coins, stamps and bank notes. Although these references may well be regarded as a permissible illustration that we are a religious people . . . , it does not follow that the Regents prayer is beyond the reach of the First Amendment. Such an approach belies the avowed purpose of the Regents which, as we have pointed out, was to commence "teaching our children" (Statement of Belief). In our view, this conflicts with the establishment clause which, under the Fourteenth Amendment, applies to the state . . .

The opinion concludes:

The inculcation of religion is a matter for the family and the church. In sponsoring a religious program, the State enters a field which it has been thought best to leave to the church alone. However salutary an underlying purpose of the requirement may be, it nonetheless gives the State a direct supervision and influence that overstep the line marking the division between church and State and cannot help but lead to a gradual erosion of the mighty bulwark erected by the First Amendment. This does not mean that the State is or should be hostile to religion—merely that the State should not invade an area where the constitutionally protected freedom is absolute and not open to the vicissitudes of legislative or judicial balancing.

THE SUPREME COURT RULES

On June 25, 1962, the Supreme Court in *Engel* v. *Vitale*,[1] rendered its opinion. Only seven justices took part in the decision since Justice Frankfurter was ill and Justice White had been appointed after the arguments in this case had been heard. The opinion was written by Justice Black. Justice Stewart was the lone dissenter.

Briefs were filed on behalf of the Attorney Generals of Arizona, Arkansas, Connecticut, Florida, Georgia, Idaho, Indiana, Kansas, Louisiana, Maryland, Mississippi, Nevada, New Hampshire, New Jersey, New Mexico, North Dakota, Pennsylvania, Rhode Island, South Carolina, South Dakota, Texas, and West Virginia who urged as *amici curiae* that the lower court decision be upheld. They were joined in this viewpoint by attorneys for the New York State Board of Regents.

Briefs were filed urging reversal by attorneys for the American Ethical Union, the American Jewish Committee, and the Synagogue Council of America.

THE OPINION OF THE COURT

After reviewing the facts and the previous legal proceedings, Justice Black immediately made clear what the Court's ruling would be:

[1] 370 U.S. 421.

We think that by using its public school system to encourage recitation of the Regents' prayer, the State of New York has adopted a practice wholly inconsistent with the Establishment Clause. There can, of course, be no doubt that New York's program of daily classroom invocation of God's blessings as prescribed in the Regents' prayer is a religious activity. It is a solemn avowal of divine faith and supplication for the blessings of the Almighty. The nature of such a prayer has always been religious. . . .

The petitioners contend among other things that the state laws requiring or permitting use of the Regents' prayer must be struck down as a violation of the Establishment Clause because that prayer was composed by governmental officials as a part of a governmental program to further religious beliefs. For this reason, petitioners argue, the State's use of the Regents' prayer in its public school system breaches the constitutional wall of separation between Church and State. We agree with that contention since we think that the constitutional prohibition against laws respecting an establishment of religion must at least mean that in this country it is no part of the business of government to compose official prayers for any group of the American people to recite as a part of a religious program carried on by government.

In support of this viewpoint, Justice Black analyzes the history of governmentally composed prayers:

It is a matter of history that this very practice of establishing governmentally composed prayers for religious services was one of the reasons which caused many of our early colonists to leave England and seek religious freedom in America. The Book of Common Prayer, which was created under governmental direction and which was approved by Acts of Parliament in 1548 and 1549, set out in minute detail the accepted form and content of prayer and other religious ceremonies to be used in the established, tax-supported Church of England. The controversies over the Book and what should be its content repeatedly threatened to disrupt the peace of that country as the accepted forms of prayer in the established church changed with the views of the particular ruler that happened to be in control at the time. Powerful groups representing some of the varying religious views of the people struggled among themselves to impress their particular views upon the Government

and obtain amendments of the Book more suitable to their respective notions of how religious services should be conducted in
order that the official religious establishment would advance their
particular religious beliefs. Other groups, lacking the necessary
political power to influence the Government on the matter, decided
to leave England and its established church and seek freedom in
America from England's governmentally ordained and supported
religion.

It is an unfortunate fact of history that when some of the very
groups which had most strenuously opposed the established Church
of England found themselves sufficiently in control of colonial governments in this country to write their own prayers into law, they
passed laws making their own religion the official religion of their
respective colonies. Indeed, as late as the time of the Revolutionary
War, there were established churches in at least eight of the thirteen
former colonies and established religions in at least four of the
other five. But the successful Revolution against English political
domination was shortly followed by intense opposition to the practice of establishing religion by law. This opposition crystallized
rapidly into an effective political force in Virginia where the
minority religious groups such as Presbyterians, Lutherans, Quakers
and Baptists had gained such strength that the adherents to the
established Episcopal Church were actually a minority themselves.
In 1785–1786, those opposed to the established Church, led by
James Madison and Thomas Jefferson, who, though themselves not
members of any of these dissenting religious groups, opposed all
religious establishments by law on grounds of principle, obtained the
enactment of the famous "Virginia Bill for Religious Liberty" by
which all religious groups were placed on an equal footing so far
as the State was concerned. Similar though less far-reaching legislation was being considered and passed in other States.

By the time of the adoption of the Constitution, our history
shows that there was a widespread awareness among many Americans of the dangers of a union of Church and State. These people
knew, some of them from bitter personal experience, that one of
the greatest dangers to the freedom of the individual to worship in
his own way lay in the Government's placing its official stamp of
approval upon one particular kind of prayer or one particular form

of religious services. They knew the anguish, hardship and bitter strife that could come when zealous religious groups struggled with one another to obtain the Government's stamp of approval from each King, Queen, or Protector that came to temporary power. The Constitution was intended to avert a part of this danger by leaving the government of this country in the hands of the people rather than in the hands of any monarch. But this safeguard was not enough. Our Founders were no more willing to let the content of their prayers and their privilege of praying whenever they pleased be influenced by the ballot box than they were to let these vital matters of personal conscience depend upon the succession of monarchs.

The purposes of the religious clauses of the First Amendment are then briefly restated:

The First Amendment was added to the Constitution to stand as a guarantee that neither the power nor the prestige of the Federal Government would be used to control, support or influence the kinds of prayer the American people can say, that the people's religions must not be subjected to the pressures of government for change each time a new political administration is elected to office. Under that Amendment's prohibition against governmental establishment of religion, as reinforced by the provisions of the Fourteenth Amendment, government in this country, be it state or federal, is without power to prescribe by law any particular form of prayer which is to be used as an official prayer in carrying on any program of governmentally sponsored religious activity.

The Regents' prayer is described as follows:

There can be no doubt that New York's state prayer program officially establishes the religious beliefs embodied in the Regents' prayer. The respondents' argument to the contrary, which is largely based upon the contention that the Regents' prayer is "non-denominational" and the fact that the program, as modified and approved by state courts, does not require all pupils to recite the prayer but permits those who wish to do so to remain silent or be excused from the room, ignores the essential nature of the program's constitutional defects. Neither the fact that the prayer may be denominationally neutral, nor the fact that its observance on the part of the students is voluntary can serve to free it from the limitations of the Establishment Clause, as it might from the Free Exercise Clause, of the First Amendment, both of which are operative against the States by virtue of the Fourteenth Amendment. Although these two clauses may in certain instances overlap, they forbid two quite different kinds of governmental encroachment upon religious freedom. The Establishment Clause, unlike the Free Exercise Clause, does not depend upon any showing of direct governmental compulsion and is violated by the enactment of laws which establish an official religion whether those laws operate directly to coerce nonobserving individuals or not. This is not to say, of course, that laws officially prescribing a particular form of religious worship do not involve coercion of such individuals. When the power, prestige and financial support of government is placed behind a particular religious belief, the indirect coercive pressure upon religious minorities to conform to the prevailing officially approved religion is plain. But the purposes underlying the Establishment Clause go much further than that. Its first and most immediate purpose rested on the belief that a union of government and religion tends to destroy government and to degrade religion. The history of governmentally established religion, both in England and in this country, showed that whenever government had allied itself with one particular form of religion, the inevitable result had been that it had incurred the hatred, disrespect and even contempt of those who held contrary beliefs . . . The New York laws officially prescribing the Regents' prayer are inconsistent both with the purposes of the Establishment Clause and with the Establishment Clause itself.

The argument that hostility toward religion would be involved in barring the Regents' Prayer is next discussed:

It has been argued that to apply the Constitution in such a way as to prohibit state laws respecting an establishment of religious services in public schools is to indicate a hostility toward religion or toward prayer. Nothing, of course, could be more wrong. The history of man is inseparable from the history of religion. And perhaps it is not too much to say that since the beginning of that history many people have devoutly believed that "More things are wrought by prayer than this world dreams of." It was doubtless largely due to men who believed this that there grew up a sentiment that caused men to leave the cross-currents of officially established state religions and religious persecution in Europe and come to this country filled with the hope that they could find a place in which they could pray when they pleased to the God of their faith in the language they chose. And there were men of this same faith in the power of prayer who led the fight for adoption of our Constitution and also for our Bill of Rights with the very guarantees of religious freedom that forbid the sort of governmental activity which New York has attempted here. These men knew that the First Amendment, which tried to put an end to governmental control of religion and of prayer, was not written to destroy either. They knew rather that it was written to quiet well-justified fears which nearly all of them felt arising out of an awareness that governments of the past had shackled men's tongues to make them speak only the religious thoughts that government wanted them to speak and to pray only to the God that government wanted them to pray to. It is neither sacrilegious nor antireligious to say that each separate government in this country should stay out of the business of writing or sanctioning official prayers and leave that purely religious function to the people themselves and to those the people choose to look to for religious guidance.

At this point a footnote generally overlooked by commentators on this decision is inserted:

There is of course nothing in the decision reached here that is inconsistent with the fact that school children and others are officially encouraged to express love for our country by reciting historical documents such as the Declaration of Independence which contain references to the Deity or by singing officially espoused anthems which include the composer's professions of faith in a Supreme Being, or with the fact that there are many manifestations in our public life of belief in God. Such patriotic or ceremonial occasions bear no true resemblance to the unquestioned religious exercise that the State of New York has sponsored in this instance.

The opinion concludes:

It is true that New York's establishment of its Regents' prayer as an officially approved religious doctrine of that State does not amount to a total establishment of one particular religious sect to the exclusion of all others—that, indeed, the governmental endorsement of that prayer seems relatively insignificant when compared to the governmental encroachments upon religion which were commonplace 200 years ago. To those who may subscribe to the view that because the Regents' official prayer is so brief and general there can be no danger to religious freedom in its governmental establishment, however, it may be appropriate to say in the words of James Madison, the author of the First Amendment:

> "(It) is proper to take alarm at the first experiment on our liberties. . . . Who does not see that the same authority which can establish Christianity, in exclusion of all other Religions, may establish with the same ease any particular sect of Christians, in exclusion of all other Sects? That the same authority which can force a citizen to contribute three pence only of his property for the support of any one establishment, may force him to conform to any other establishment in all cases whatsoever?"

The judgment of the Court of Appeals of New York is reversed and the cause remanded for further proceedings not inconsistent with this opinion.

JUSTICE DOUGLAS' CONCURRING OPINION

Justice Douglas went somewhat further than the Court. He began:

It is customary in deciding a constitutional question to treat it in its narrowest form . . . The point for decision is whether the Government can constitutionally finance a religious exercise. Our system at the federal and state levels is presently honeycombed with such financing. Nevertheless, I think it is an unconstitutional undertaking whatever form it takes.

At this point in a footnote the following quotation from Fellman's *The Limits of Freedom* is included:

There are many "aids" to religion in this country at all levels of government. To mention but a few at the federal level, one might begin by observing that the First Congress, which wrote the First Amendment, provided for chaplains in both Houses in the armed services. There is compulsory chapel at the service academies, and religious services are held in federal hospitals and prisons. The President issues religious proclamations. The Bible is used for the administration of oaths. NYA and WPA funds were available to parochial schools during the depression. Veterans receiving money under the "G.I." Bill of 1944 could attend denominational schools to which payments were made directly by the government. During World War II, federal money was contributed to denominational schools for the training of nurses. The benefits of the National School Lunch Act are available to students in private as well as public schools. The Hospital Survey and Construction Act of 1946 specifically made money available to nonpublic hospitals. The slogan "In God We Trust" is used by the Treasury Department, and Congress recently added God to the pledge of allegiance. There is Bible-reading in the schools of the District of Columbia, and religious instruction is given in the District's National Training School for Boys. Religious organizations are exempt from the federal income tax and are granted postal privileges. Up to defined limits —15 per cent of the adjusted gross income of individuals and 5 per cent of the net income of corporations—contributions to religious organizations are deductible for federal income tax purposes. There are no limits to the deductibility of gifts and bequests to religious institutions made under the federal gift and estate tax laws. This list of federal "aids" could easily be expanded, and of course there is a long list in each state.

Justice Douglas' opinion then continues:

Plainly, our Bill of Rights would not permit a State or the Federal Government to adopt an official prayer and penalize anyone who would not utter it. This, however, is not that case, for there is no element of compulsion or coercion in New York's regulation . . . As I read this regulation, a child is free to stand or not stand, to recite or not recite, without fear of reprisal or even comment by the teacher or any other school official.

It is then stated that this case is not governed by the *McCollum* ruling because:

. . . But New York's prayer is of a character that does not involve any element of proselytizing as in the *McCollum* case.

The opinion next discusses the nature of the question presented in this case:

The question presented by this case is therefore an extremely narrow one. It is whether New York oversteps the bounds when it finances a religious exercise.

What New York does on the opening of its public schools is what we do when we open court. Our Crier has from the beginning announced the convening of the Court and then added "God save the United States and this Honorable Court." That utterance is a supplication, a prayer in which we, the judges, are free to join, but which we need not recite any more than the students need recite the New York prayer.

What New York does on the opening of its public schools is what each House of Congress does at the opening of each day's business. Reverend Frederick B. Harris is Chaplain of the Senate; Reverend Bernard Braskamp is Chaplain of the House. Guest chaplains of various denominations also officiate.

In New York the teacher who leads in prayer is on the public payroll; and the time she takes seems minuscule as compared with the salaries appropriated by state legislatures and Congress for chaplains to conduct prayers in the legislative halls. Only a bare fraction of the teacher's time is given to reciting this short 22-word prayer, about the same amount of time that our Crier spends announcing the opening of our sessions and offering a prayer for this Court. Yet for me the principle is the same, no matter how briefly the prayer is said, for in each of the instances given the person praying is a public official on the public payroll, performing a religious exercise in a governmental institution.

At this point in a footnote Justice Douglas points out that the taxpayers would not have legal standing in court to raise the issue but that this does not really affect the legality of the procedures described. He continues:

At the same time I cannot say that to authorize this prayer is to establish a religion in the strictly historic meaning of those words. A religion is not established in the usual sense merely by letting those who chose to do so say the prayer that the public school teacher leads. Yet once government finances a religious exercise it inserts a divisive influence into our communities.

The doctrine laid down in *Everson* is questioned by Justice Douglas:

My problem today would be uncomplicated but for *Everson v. Board of Education*, 330 U.S. 1, 17, which allowed taxpayers' money to be used to pay "the bus fares of parochial school pupils as a part of a general program under which" the fares of pupils attending public and other schools were also paid. The *Everson* case seems in retrospect to be out of line with the First Amendment. Its result is appealing, as it allows aid to be given to needy children. Yet by the same token, public funds could be used to satisfy other needs of children in parochial schools—lunches, books, and tuition being obvious examples.

Justice Douglas quotes with approval from Justice Rutledge's dissenting opinion in the Everson case and concludes his opinion by stating:

What New York does with this prayer is a break with that tradition. I therefore join the Court in reversing the judgment below.

JUSTICE STEWART'S DISSENTING OPINION

Justice Stewart filed a vigorous dissent which opened with the statement:

A local school board in New York has provided that those pupils who wish to do so may join in a brief prayer at the beginning of each school day, acknowledging their dependence upon God and asking His blessing upon them and upon their parents, their teachers, and country. The Court today decides that in permitting this brief nondenominational prayer the school board has violated the Constitution of the United States. I think this decision is wrong.

The Court does not hold, nor could it, that New York has interfered with the free exercise of anybody's religion. For the state courts have made clear that those who object to reciting the prayer must be entirely free of any compulsion to do so, including any "embarrassments and pressures." Cf. *West Virginia State Board of Education* v. *Barnette*, 319 U.S. 624. But the Court says that in permitting school children to say this simple prayer, the New York authorities have established "an official religion."

With all respect, I think the Court has misapplied a great constitutional principle. I cannot see how an "official religion" is established by letting those who want to say a prayer say it. On the contrary, I think to deny the wish of these school children to join in reciting this prayer is to deny them the opportunity of sharing in the spiritual heritage of our Nation.

The Court's historical review of the quarrels over the Book of Common Prayer in England throws no light for me on the issue before us in this case. England had then and has now an established church. Equally unenlightening, I think, is the history of the early establishment and later rejection of an official church in our own States. For we deal here not with the establishment of a state church, which would, of course, be constitutionally impermissible, but with whether school children who want to begin their day by joining in prayer must be prohibited from doing so. Moreover, I think that the Court's task, in this as in all areas of constitutional adjudication, is not responsibly aided by the uncritical invocation of metaphors like the "wall of separation," a phrase nowhere to be found in the Constitution. What is relevant to the issue here is not the history of an established church in sixteenth century England or in eighteenth century America, but the history of the religious tradition of our people, reflected in countless practices of the institutions and officials of our government.

Justice Stewart then reviews various religious manifestations in the opening of the Supreme Court's sessions, the Houses of Congress, etc., and includes in a footnote statements by a number of Presidents asking the protection and help of God. He further cites the third verse of the "Star Spangled Banner," the phrase "under God" in the Pledge of Allegiance, the 1952 Congressional resolution calling on the President to proclaim an annual "Day of Prayer" and the inscription on our coinage of the words "In God We Trust." Justice Stewart then comments in a footnote:

I am at a loss to understand the Court's unsupported *ipse dixit* that these official expressions of religious faith in and reliance upon a Supreme Being "bear no true resemblance to the unquestioned religious exercise that the State of New York has sponsored in this instance." . . . I can hardly think that the Court means to say that the First Amendment imposes a lesser restriction upon the Federal Government than does the Fourteenth Amendment upon the States. Or is the Court suggesting that the Constitution permits judges and Congressmen and Presidents to join in prayer, but prohibits school children from doing so?

The opinion concludes:

I do not believe that this Court, or the Congress, or the President has by the actions and practices I have mentioned established an "official religion" in violation of the Constitution. And I do not believe the State of New York has done so in this case. What each has done has been to recognize and to follow the deeply entrenched and highly cherished spiritual traditions of our Nation—traditions which come down to us from those who almost two hundred years ago avowed their "firm Reliance on the Protection of divine Providence" when they proclaimed the freedom and independence of this brave world.
I dissent.

In this case it was decided that the requirement of the recital of a state-composed prayer in a public school classroom was in violation of the Establishment Clause of the First Amendment.

SUMMARY

1. The New York State Board of Regents composed a "nonsectarian" prayer and recommended its use in public school classrooms.

2. In *Engel* v. *Vitale* the recitation of this prayer was attacked as a violation of the Establishment Clause of the First Amendment.

3. Three New York State courts upheld the validity of the school board regulation requiring the recitation of the prayer, principally on the basis of the provision permitting nonparticipation by children whose parents objected to such recital.

4. The Supreme Court of the United States reversed these rulings and held the recital of this prayer to be a violation of the Establishment Clause.

5. The ruling of the Court was confined to a state-written prayer but Justice Douglas' concurring opinion was much broader in its application. Justice Stewart dissented.

6. Considerable controversial public reaction resulted from this decision.

CHAPTER 8

ENGEL v. VITALE
CLARIFIED AND EXPANDED

During the October, 1962, term three cases that involved questions quite similar to those posed in the *Engel* case reached the Supreme Court of the United States. The action of the Court in these cases can best be understood against the background of short reviews of the facts involved.

THE PENNSYLVANIA CASE

The first of these cases, *Schempp v. School District of Abington Township*, was heard by a Federal District Court, sitting in Pennsylvania, in 1959. In cases where the constitutionality under the United States Constitution of a state statute is in question a three-Judge Court is convened and that was done here. This was an action to restrain the enforcement of a Pennsylvania statute providing for the reading of ten verses of the Holy Bible by teachers and students, without comment, at the opening of each school day. This action was brought in behalf of three pupils by their Unitarian parent. The lower court held that such reading constituted a religious ceremony and that the statute thus violated the First and Fourteenth Amendments of the United States Constitution. Before discussing the reasoning employed by the District Court in reaching this decision, several interesting factual sidelights may be noted:

1. One of the Schempp children was graduated from high school between the time of the filing and the hearing of this case. In *Doremus* v. *Board of Education*, the Supreme Court in 1951 refused to pass on the constitutionality of a Bible reading statute in New Jersey on the ground that the case had become moot, because the child in whose behalf the action had been brought had been graduated in the course of the litigation. In the *Schempp* case, there were two younger children still in school, the youngest being in the seventh grade in 1959.

2. The Lord's Prayer was said after the reading of the Bible verses, but the issue of the constitutionality or lack of it of reciting this prayer was not raised in this case.

3. The state statute did not define the term "Holy Bible." In the Abington schools the St. James version was used.

4. In his Junior year the oldest Schempp child had been permitted to spend the period devoted to Bible reading in a counselor's office. This was after he had read the Koran during the Bible reading and had refused to stand during the recitation of the Lord's Prayer. In his Senior year, however, he was required to remain in the classroom during the Bible reading. The other Schempp children, apparently, did not raise this issue.

THE CONTENTION OF THE SCHOOL DISTRICT

In deciding the case the lower court said in part:

The defendants assert a position which is diametrically opposed to that of the plaintiffs. They contend in substance that a reading without comment of ten verses of the "Holy Bible" at the opening of each school day does not affect, favor, or establish a religion or prohibit the free exercise thereof; that freedom of religion or of conscience does not include a right to practice one's beliefs or disbeliefs concerning the Bible by preventing others from hearing it read in the public schools. They contend also that reading without comment of ten verses of the "Holy Bible" of whatever version, is a substantial aid in developing the minds and morals of school children and that the State has a constitutional right to employ such practices in its educational program. They assert as well that the custom of saying the Lord's Prayer does not concern an establishment of religion nor violate the religious conscience of pupil or parent. Finally, they contend that there is no compulsion upon the plaintiffs in respect to religious observances and that they have not shown that they have been deprived of any constitutional right.

Rejecting these contentions, the Court continues:

Inasmuch as the verses of the Bible address themselves to, or are premised upon, the recognition of God, the Bible is essentially a religious work. To characterize the Bible as a work of art, of literary and historical significance and to refuse to admit its essential character as a religious document would seem to us to be unrealistic.

Continuing, the Court says:

The daily reading of the Bible buttressed with the authority of the State, and, more importantly, to children, backed with the authority of their teachers, can hardly do less than inculcate or promote the inculcation of various religious doctrines in childish minds.

Rejecting further the arguments offered by the defendants, the Court adds:

The reading of the Bible without comment, the defendants assert, permits each listener to interpret what he hears in the fashion he desires, and that, therefore, there is no inculcation of religion. This argument fails for two reasons. First, it either ignores the essentially religious nature of the Bible, or assumes that its religious quality can be disregarded by the listener. This too much to ignore and too much to assume. . . .

The Court characterizes the morning exercises as "devotional" and said that whether or not it was a "religious ceremony":

. . . a state supported practice of daily reading from that essentially religious text in the public school is, we believe, within the proscription of the First Amendment.

In closing, the Court points out that the compulsory school attendance laws, "put the children in the path of compulsion."

THE PENNSYLVANIA LAW IS AMENDED

Immediately after this decision and while the case was being carried to the Supreme Court, the Pennsylvania legislature passed an amendment to the Bible-reading statute providing that pupils wishing to be excused would not be required to take part in the Bible reading.

SUPREME COURT OF THE UNITED STATES ACTS

When the Supreme Court reached the case in October of 1960, (364 U.S. 298), it remanded the case to the District Court in the light of the amended Pennsylvania statute. This action was interpreted by some (including, as we shall see, the highest court in Maryland) as indicating the Supreme Court's feeling that the constitutionality of the Pennsylvania Bible-reading requirement had been affected by the legislative action in amending the statute. This however, was twenty months before the decision in the *Engel* case.

REHEARING IN THE DISTRICT COURT

On the retrial of the *Schempp* case, the plaintiff contended that despite the amendment the law was still constitutionally objectionable. He did not want his children excused because:

1. They would be labelled as "odd balls";
2. Other children lump all particular religious differences as atheism, which is often associated with Communism;
3. Since school announcements were usually made immediately after the ceremony, his children might miss these; and
4. If his children had to stand outside of their homerooms during the ceremony, there would be an implication of punishment for bad conduct.

The Court held that whether or not children might be excused did not alter the fact that religious ceremonies were being held in public school buildings under authority of local school authorities. In declaring such practices unconstitutional even under the amended statute, it concluded:

The record demonstrates that it was the intention of the General Assembly of the Commonwealth of Pennsylvania to introduce a religious ceremony into the public schools of the Commonwealth.

The case was again carried to the Supreme Court, which accepted jurisdiction in October of 1962.

THE BALTIMORE CASE

The second case in which the Supreme Court accepted jurisdiction was *Murray v. Curlett*, which was decided by the Court of Appeals of the State of Maryland in April, 1962. In this case the complaint was based on the alleged unconstitutionality of a 1905 school board ruling pertaining to opening exercises in public schools wherein the Holy Bible was read and the Lord's Prayer recited. This Baltimore city ruling was amended in 1960 to provide that:

Any child shall be excused from participating in the opening exercises or from attending the opening exercises upon written request of his parent or guardian.

THE STATE COURT'S RULING

The Court of Appeals found by a majority of 4 to 3 that this rule did not violate the constitutional rights of the plaintiff, saying in part:

We think that neither constitutional provision is violated, for, as we see it, neither the First nor the Fourteenth Amendment was intended to stifle all rapport between religion and government.

The Court's reasoning was based on two premises:

1. That the case fell somewhere between the *McCollum* case, in which the Supreme Court had held in 1948 that a provision for released time from public school attendance for religious instruction on the school premises was constitutionally objectionable, and the *Zorach* case, in which the Supreme Court held three years later that a provision for dismissal time was not objectionable when the religious instruction was given away from the school premises.

2. That the Supreme Court's action in remanding the *Schempp* case to the District Court in the light of the amendment to the Pennsylvania law, indicated that Court's approval of Bible reading when there was, as in the instant case, provision for excusing children who did not wish to participate.

THE DISSENTING VIEW IN THE STATE COURT

The dissenting minority of three justices after citing "the wall of separation between Church and State," referred to in the *Everson* case, 330 U.S. 1 (1946), took the position that on the basis of its facts this case fell squarely within the prohibition of the *McCollum* case.

In speaking of the provisions made for excusing participation, the dissenting Justices said that they felt:

A hesitancy to expose a child to the suspicions of his fellows and to losing caste with them . . . will tend to cause the surrender of his and his parents' religious or non-religious convictions and will thus tend to put the hand of the State into the scales on the side of a particular religion which is supported by the prescribed exercises.

THE ISSUES INVOLVED

In addition to raising the issues that were involved in the *Schempp* case, the *Murray* case squarely presented the issue of the constitutionality of the recital of the Lord's Prayer in public school classrooms.

The Supreme Court also accepted jurisdiction in this case.

THE FLORIDA CASE

Perhaps the most potentially explosive case was *Chamberlin v. Dade County Board of Public Instruction*, because of the number of issues raised by the complaints. However, by the time these cases reached the Florida Supreme Court, where a decision was rendered (143 So. 2d 21) in June of 1962, as we shall see, the issue was no longer joined on a number of the points originally raised. The original complaints sought to have the following school practices declared to be in contravention of the United States Constitution:

1. The regular reading of the Bible
2. Comments on the Bible passages read
3. Distribution of sectarian literature to school children
4. After-school hours Bible instruction in school buildings
5. Regular recitation of the Lord's Prayer, Grace, and other sectarian prayers
6. Religious observances of Christmas, Hanukkah, and Easter, including instruction in the dogma of the Nativity and the Resurrection
7. Display of religious symbols
8. Baccalaureate programs
9. Conducting a religious census of pupils

10. Use of religious tests for employment and promotion of school employees

The trial court after a "prolonged trial and the taking of some 1400 pages of testimony," granted a portion of the relief asked by forbidding the following: (1) Sectarian comments on the Bible; (2) Use of school premises for after-school-hours Bible instruction; (3) Exhibition of films with religious content; and (4) Religious observance in public schools of Christmas, Hanukkah, and Easter holidays. Since the school board did not appeal these rulings, the Florida Supreme Court was not given the opportunity to pass upon these issues. It follows that these issues also were not before the Supreme Court of the United States when it was asked to accept jurisdiction of this case. Some rather interesting questions were, therefore, left up in the air even after the action of the Florida Supreme Court.

RULING OF THE FLORIDA SUPREME COURT

The Florida court held that Bible reading, recitation of the Lord's Prayer, singing of religious hymns, and the holding of baccalaureate services were unobjectionable from a constitutional standpoint. It further affirmed the finding of the trial court that the only religious symbols displayed were ". . . works of art created by the school children and were displayed on a temporary basis and not of a permanent nature." It agreed that under these facts there was no violation of any constitutional provision by such display. The court further approved of the lower court's finding that there was insufficient evidence to sustain plaintiffs' complaints regarding a religious census of school children and the imposition of religious tests for the employment and promotion of school personnel. Somewhere along the line the matter of the "distribution of sectarian literature to school children" seems to have been lost, as no mention is made of it in the decision.

THE FLORIDA SUPREME COURT IS "NOT IMPRESSED"

In support of its ruling the Florida court used the following language in speaking of the definition of the Establishment Clause of the First Amendment given by the Supreme Court of the United States in *Everson*, where that Court said that the clause was intended to erect "a wall of separation between Church and State";

We are not impressed with the language quoted as being definitive of the "establishment clause." It goes far beyond the purpose and intent of the authors and beyond any reasonable application to the practical facts of every day life in this country.

Further commenting on relevant Supreme Court decisions, the Florida court continued:

It is beyond the realm of possibility for this court to reconcile our conception of the First Amendment with the too broad language of the several decisions relied upon by the plaintiff. Nor have we been able to reconcile the several retreats, modifications, and hair-splitting distinctions written in these opinions and made to accommodate varying statements of fact.

The Court holds that where there was no compulsion (in this case a regulation of the Dade County Board of Public Instruction required that pupils be excused from attendance at religious ceremonies upon the request of their parents) there can be no violation of the Establishment Clause of the First Amendment. The opinion goes on to say that in this court's opinion there is no valid or real distinction in principle or in substance between this case and the *Zorach* case. The opinion continues:

It does not appear . . . that there is any serious contention that the children of the plaintiffs have suffered or will suffer any measurable psychological trauma as a consequence of the reading of the Bible, either in or out of their presence. Rather, it seems that this is just another case in which the tender sensibilities of certain minorities are sought to be protected against the alleged harsh laws and customs enacted and established by the more rugged pioneers of the Nation. In the instant case we are told that the primary objects of solicitude are the children of the plaintiffs, atheists, Unitarians, and Jews, which children, although not required to be present at the time, will, so it is said, suffer some supposedly irreparable emotional stress if their classmates are permitted to hear the Bible read.

In further support of its views the court says:

The concept of God has been and is so interwoven into every aspect of American institutions that to attack this concept is to threaten the very fiber of our existence as a nation.

The minority and majority are both denied the privilege of disrupting the life of others because of some hypersensitivity or fractious temperament.

We are sensible of the extent to which the sophisticacies of agnosticism have gained credence. And we acknowledge the trend toward the preference of minorities over the majority and toward the rights of the majority which never seem to suffer psychological trauma, to yield up its cherished customs and rights.

The court comments on the fact that all children must under the Florida statute be taught about the history, doctrines, objectives, and techniques of Communism and says:

Thus the school board affords the atheists the freedom of hearing or not hearing the Bible read while it requires that all students, without choice, be taught the facts of Communism, the antithesis of the Bible.

THE SUPREME COURT RULES

On June 17, 1963, the Supreme Court of the United States ruled on the *Schempp* and *Murray* cases in a single set of opinions. On the same day the Court in a brief ruling accepted jurisdiction of the Florida case and then summarily remanded it to the Florida state courts with instructions to reconsider their rulings in the light of the *Schempp* and *Murray* decisions, using the following language:

The judgment is vacated and the case is remanded to the Supreme Court of Florida for further consideration in the light of *Murray* v. *Curlett* and *School District and Abington Township* v. *Schempp* . . . , both decided this day.

The opinion of the Court in the *Schempp* and *Murray* cases was delivered by Justice Clark. Concurring opinions were written by Justices Douglas, Brennan, and Goldberg. Justice Harlan joined in the opinion written by Justice Goldberg. Justice Stewart, alone, dissented.

THE OPINION OF THE COURT

Justice Clark in his opinion made clear in the first paragraph that the ruling was against the permissibility of the practices about which the issue had been raised:

Once again we are called upon to consider the scope of the provision of the First Amendment to the United States Constitution which declares that "Congress shall make no law respecting an establishment of religion, or prohibiting the free exercise thereof. . . ." These companion cases present the issue in the context of state action requiring that schools begin each day with readings from the Bible. While raising the basic questions under slightly different factual situations, the cases permit of joint treatment. In light of the history of the First Amendment and of our cases interpreting and applying its requirements, we hold that the practices at issue and the laws requiring them are unconstitutional under the Establishment Clause, as applied to the states through the Fourteenth Amendment.

After reviewing the facts involved and the previous legal proceedings in these cases Justice Clark continues:

It is true that religion has been closely identified with our history and government. As we said in *Engel v. Vitale* . . ., "The history of man is inseparable from the history of religion. And . . . since the beginning of that history many people have devoutly believed that 'More things are wrought by prayer than this world dreams of.'" In *Zorach v. Clauson* . . ., we gave specific recognition to the proposition that "we are a religious people whose institutions presuppose a Supreme Being." The fact that the Founding Fathers believed devotedly that there was a God and that the unalienable rights of man were rooted in Him is clearly evidenced in their writings, from the Mayflower Compact to the Constitution itself. This background is evidence today in our public life through the continuance in our oaths of office from the Presidency to the Alderman of the final supplication "So help me God." Likewise each House of Congress provides through its Chaplain an opening prayer, and the sessions of this Court are declared open by the crier in a short ceremony, the final phrase of which invokes the grace of God. Again there are such manifestations in our military forces, where those of our citizens who are under the restrictions of military service wish to engage in voluntary worship. Indeed only last year an official survey of the country indicated that 64% of our people have church membership . . . , while less than 3% profess no religion whatever. . . . It can be truly said, therefore, that today, as in the beginning, our national life reflects a religious people who in the words of Madison are "earnestly praying, as . . . in duty bound, that the Supreme Lawgiver of the Universe . . . guide them into every measure which may be worthy of his . . . blessing. . . ." . . . This is not to say, however, that religion has been so identified with our history and our government that religious freedom is not likewise as strongly imbedded in our public and private life. Nothing but the most telling of personal experiences in religious persecution suffered by our forebears, . . . could have planted our heritage. It is true that this liberty frequently was not realized by the colonists, but this is readily accountable by their close ties to the Mother Country. However, the views of Madison and Jefferson, preceded by Roger Williams, came to be incorporated not only in the Federal Constitution but likewise in those of most of our States. This freedom to worship was indispensable in a country whose people came from the four quarters of the earth and brought with them a diversity of religious opinion. Today authorities list 83 separate religious bodies each with memberships exceeding 50,000, existing among our people, as well as innumerable smaller groups. . . .

Reviewing previous rulings, Justice Clark states:

. . . this court has decisively settled that the First Amendment's mandate that "Congress shall make no law respecting an establishment of religion or prohibiting the free exercise thereof" has been made wholly applicable to the states by the Fourteenth Amendment.

. . . this Court has rejected unequivocally the contention that the establishment clause forbids only governmental preference of one religion over another.

The opinion continues after expanding on these two statements:

While none of the parties to either of these cases has questioned these basic conclusions of the Court, both of which have been long established, recognized and consistently reaffirmed, others continue to question their history, logic and efficacy. Such contentions, in the light of the consistent interpretation in cases of this Court, seem entirely untenable and of value only as academic exercises.

After further review of related previous cases decided by the Supreme Court, Justice Clark states:

The wholesome "neutrality" of which this Court's cases speak thus stems from a recognition of the teachings of history that powerful sects or groups might bring about a fusion of governmental and religious functions or a concert or dependency of one upon the other to the end that official support of the State or Federal Government would be placed behind the tenets of one or of all orthodoxies. This the Establishment Clause prohibits. And a further reason for neutrality is found in the Free Exercise Clause, which recognizes the value of religious training, teaching and observance and, more particularly, the right of every person to freely choose his own course thereto, free of any compulsion from the state. This the Free Exercise Clause guarantees. Thus, as we have seen, the two clauses may overlap. As we have indicated, the Establishment Clause has been directly considered by this Court eight times in the past score of years and, with only one Justice dissenting on the point, it has consistently held that the clause withdrew all legislative power respecting religious belief or the expression thereof. The test may be stated as follows: What are the purpose and the primary effect of the enactment? If either is the advancement or inhibition of religion then the enactment exceeds the scope of legislative power as circumscribed by the Constitution. That is to say that to withstand the strictures of the Establishment Clause there must be a secular legislative purpose and a primary effect that neither advances nor inhibits religion. . . . The Free Exercise Clause, likewise considered many times here, withdraws from legislative power, state and federal, the exertion of any restraint on the free exercise of religion. Its purpose is to secure religious liberty in the individual by prohibiting any invasions thereof by civil authority. Hence it is necessary in a free exercise case for one to show the coercive effect of the enactment as it operates against him in the practice of his religion. The distinction between the two clauses is apparent—a violation of the Free Exercise Clause is predicated on coercion while the Establishment Clause violation need not be so attended.

Applying the Establishment Clause principles to the cases at bar we find that the States are requiring the selection and reading at the opening of the school day of verses from the Holy Bible and the recitation of the Lord's Prayer by the students in unison. These exercises are prescribed as part of the curricular activities of students who are required by law to attend school. They are held in the school buildings under the supervision and with the participation of teachers employed in those schools. None of these factors, other than compulsory school attendance, was present in the program upheld in Zorach v. Clauson. The trial court in No. 142, Schempp, has found that such an opening exercise is a religious ceremony and was intended by the State to be so. We agree with the trial court's finding as to the religious character of the exercises. Given that finding, the exercises and the law requiring them are in violation of the Establishment Clause.

There is no such specific finding as to the religious character of the exercises in No. 119 *Murray*, and the State contends (as does the State in No. 142 *Schempp*), that the program is an effort to extend its benefits to all public school children without regard to their religious belief. Included within its secular purposes, it says, are the promotion of moral values, the contradiction to the materialistic trends of our times, the perpetuation of our institutions and the teaching of literature. . . . But even if its purpose is not strictly religious, it is sought to be accomplished through readings, without comment, from the Bible. Surely the place of the Bible as an instrument of religion cannot be gainsaid, and the State's recognition of the pervading religious character of the ceremony is evident from the rule's specific permission of the alternative use of the Catholic Douay version as well as the recent amendment permitting nonattendance at the exercises. None of these factors is consistent with the contention that the Bible is here used either as an instrument for nonreligious moral inspiration or as a reference for the teaching of secular subjects.

The conclusion follows that in both cases the laws require religious exercises and such exercises are being conducted in direct violation of the rights of the appellees and petitioners. Nor are these required exercises mitigated by the fact that individual students may absent themselves upon parental request, for that fact furnishes no defense to a claim of unconstitutionality under the Establishment Clause. . . . Further, it is no defense to urge that the religious practices here may be relatively minor encroachments on the First Amendment. The breach of neutrality that is today a trickling stream may all too soon become a raging torrent. . . .

It is insisted that unless these religious exercises are permitted a "religion of secularism" is established in the schools. We agree of course that the State may not establish a "religion of secularism" in the sense of affirmatively opposing or showing hostility to religion, thus "preferring those who believe in no religion over those who do believe." . . . We do not agree, however, that this decision in any sense has that effect. In addition, it might well be said that one's education is not complete without a study of comparative

religion or the history of religion and its relationship to the advancement of civilization. It certainly may be said that the Bible is
worthy of study for its literary and historic qualities. Nothing we
have said here indicates that such study of the Bible or of religion,
when presented objectively as part of a secular program of education, may not be effected consistent with the First Amendment.
But the exercises here do not fall into those categories. They are
religious exercises, required by the States in violation of the command of the First Amendment that the Government maintain
strict neutrality, neither aiding nor opposing religion.

Finally, we cannot accept that the concept of neutrality, which
does not permit a State to require a religious exercise even with the
consent of the majority of those affected, collides with the majority's right to free exercise of religion. While the Free Exercise
clause clearly prohibits the use of state action to deny the rights
of free exercise to anyone, it has never meant that a majority could
use the machinery of the State to practice its beliefs. . . .

In conclusion the opinion states:

The place of religion in our society is an exalted one, achieved
through a long tradition of reliance on the home, the church, and
the inviolable citadel of the individual heart and mind. We have
come to recognize through bitter experience that it is not within
the power of government to invade that citadel, whether its purpose or effect be to aid or oppose, to advance or retard. In the relationship between man and religion, the State is firmly committed
to a position of neutrality. Though the application of that rule
requires interpretation of a delicate sort, the rule itself is clearly and
concisely stated in the words of the First Amendment. . . .

JUSTICE DOUGLAS'
CONCURRING OPINION

Justice Douglas' concurring opinion was quite concise
and is given here in full except that footnotes are omitted.

I join the opinion of the Court and add a few words in explanation. While the Free Exercise Clause of the First Amendment is

written in terms of what the State may not require of the individual, the Establishment Clause, serving the same goal of individual religious freedom, is written in different terms. Establishment of a religion can be achieved in several ways. The church and state can be one; the church may control the state or the state may control the church; or the relationship may take one of several possible forms of a working arrangement between the two bodies. Under all of these arrangements the church typically has a place in the state's budget, and church law usually governs such matters as baptism, marriage, divorce and separation, at least for its members and sometimes for the entire body politic. Education, too, is usually high on the priority list of church interests. In the past schools were often made the exclusive responsibility of the church. Today in some state-church countries the state runs the public schools, but compulsory religious exercises are often required of some or all students. Thus, under the agreement Franco made with the Holy See when he came to power in Spain, "The Church regained its place in the national budget. It insists on baptising all children and has made the catechism obligatory in state schools."

The vice of all such arrangements under the Establishment Clause is that a state is lending its assistance to a church's efforts to gain and keep adherents. Under the First Amendment it is strictly a matter for the individual and his church as to what church he will belong to and how much support, in the way of belief, time, activity or money he will give to it. . . .

In these cases we have no coercive religious exercise aimed at making the students conform. The prayers announced are not compulsory, though some may think they have that indirect effect because the nonconformist student may be induced to participate for fear of being called an "odd-ball." But that coercion, if it be present, has not been shown; so the vices of the present regimes are different. These regimes violate the Establishment Clause in two different ways. In each case the State is conducting a religious exercise; and, as the Court holds, that cannot be done without violating the "neutrality" required of the State by the balance of power between individual, church and state that has been struck by the First Amendment. But the Establishment Clause is not limited to precluding the State itself from conducting religious exercises. It also forbids the State to employ its facilities or funds in a way that gives any Church, or all churches, greater strength in our society than it would have by relying on its members alone. Thus, the present regimes must fall under that clause for the additional reason that public funds, though small in amount, are being used to promote a religious exercise. Through the mechanism of the State, all of the people are being required to finance a religious exercise that only some of the people want and that violates the sensibilities of others. *The most effective way to establish any institution is to finance it; and this truth is reflected in the appeals by church groups for public funds to finance their religious schools.* Financing a church either in its strictly religious activities or in its other activities is equally unconstitutional, as I understand the Establishment Clause. Budgets for one activity may be technically separable from budgets for others. But the institution is an inseparable whole, a living organism, which is strengthened in proselytizing when it is strengthened in any department by contributions from other than its own members.

Such contributions may not be made by the State even in a minor degree without violating the Establishment Clause. It is not the amount of public funds expended; as this case illustrated, it is the use to which public funds are put that is controlling. For the First Amendment does not say that some forms of establishment are allowed; it says that "no law respecting an establishment of religion" shall be made. What may not be done directly may not be done indirectly lest the Establishment Clause become a mockery.

JUSTICE BRENNAN'S CONCURRING OPINION

Justice Brennan's 77-page concurring opinion began:

Almost a century and a half ago, John Marshall, in *McCulloch v. Maryland*, enjoined: ". . . we must never forget, that it is a *constitution* we are expounding." . . . The Court's historic duty to expound the meaning of the Constitution has encountered few issues more intricate or more demanding than that of the relationship between religion and the public schools. Since undoubtedly we are "a religious people whose institutions presuppose a Supreme

Being," . . . deep feelings are aroused when aspects of that relationship are claimed to violate the injunction of the First Amendment that government may make "no law respecting an establishment of religion, or prohibiting the free exercise thereof. . . ."
Americans regard the public schools as a most vital civic inistitution
for the preservation of a democratic form of government. It is
therefore understandable that the constitutional prohibitions en-
counter their severest test when they are sought to be applied in
the classroom. Nevertheless, it is this Court's inescapable duty to
declare whether exercises in the public schools of the States, such
as those of Pennsylvania and Maryland questioned here, are involvements of religion in public institutions of a kind which offends
the First and Fourteenth Amendments.

Justice Brennan continues by discussing the dividing line
between secular and sectarian matters:

When John Locke ventured in 1689, "I esteem it above all
things necessary to distinguish exactly the business of civil government from that of religion and to settle the just bounds that lie
between the one and the other," he anticipated the necessity which
would be thought by the Framers to require the adoption of the
First Amendment, but not the difficulty that would be experienced
in defining those "just bounds." The fact is that the line which
separates the secular from the sectarian in American life is elusive.
The difficulty of defining the boundary with precision inheres in a
paradox central to our scheme of liberty. While our institutions
reflect a firm conviction that we are a religious people, those institutions by solemn constitutional injunction may not officially involve religion in such a way as to prefer, discriminate against, or
oppress, a particular sect or religion. Equally the Constitution en-
joins those involvements of religious with secular institutions which
(a) serve the essentially religious activities of religious institutions;
(b) employ the organs of government for essentially religious purpose; or (c) use essentially religious means to serve governmental
ends where secular means would suffice. The constitutional mandate expresses a deliberate and considered judgment that such
matters are to be left to the conscience of the citizen, and declares
as a basic postulate of the relation between the citizen and his
government that "the rights of conscience are, in their nature, of

peculiar delicacy, and will bear little the gentlest touch of governmental hand . . ."

I join fully in the opinion and the judgment of the Court. I see
no escape from the conclusion that the exercises called in question
in these two cases violate the constitutional mandate.

It is then stated that the holding of *Engel* v. *Vitale* compels this holding. The opinion continues:

While it is my view that not every involvement of religion in
public life is unconstitutional, I consider the exercises at bar a form
of involvement which clearly violates the Establishment Clause.

After examining the historical foundations of the First
Amendment's provisions concerning religion, Justice Brennan
continues by stating:

A too literal question for the advice of the Founding Fathers
upon the issues of these cases seems to me futile and misdirected
for several reasons: First, on our precise problem the historical
record is at best ambiguous, and statements can readily be found
to support either side of the proposition. The ambiguity of history
is understandable if we recall the nature of the problems uppermost
in the thinking of the statesmen who fashioned the religious
guarantees; they were concerned with far more flagrant intrusions
of government into the realm of religion than any that our century
has witnessed. While it is clear to me that the Framers meant the
Establishment Clause to prohibit more than the creation of an
established Federal church such as existed in England, I have no
doubt that, in their preoccupation with the imminent question of
established churches, they gave no distinct consideration to the
particular question whether the clause also forbade devotional
exercises in public institutions. Second, the structure of American
education has greatly changed since the First Amendment was
adopted. In the context of our modern emphasis upon public education available to all citizens, any views of the eighteenth century
as to whether the exercises at bar are an "establishment" offer little
aid to decision. Education, as the Framers knew it, was in the main
confined to private schools more often than not under strictly
sectarian supervision. Only gradually did control of education pass

largely to public officials. It would, therefore, hardly be significant if the fact was that the nearly universal devotional exercises in the schools of the young Republic did not provoke criticism; even today religious ceremonies in church-supported private schools are constitutionally unobjectionable.

Third, our religious composition makes us a vastly more diverse people than were our forefathers. They knew differences chiefly among Protestant sects. Today the Nation is far more heterogenous religiously, including as it does substantial minorities not only of Catholics and Jews but as well of those who worship according to no version of the Bible and those who worship no God at all. . . . In the face of such profound changes, practices which may have been objectionable to no one in the time of Jefferson and Madison may today be highly offensive to many persons, the deeply devout and the nonbelievers alike.

Whatever Jefferson or Madison would have thought of Bible reading or the recital of the Lord's Prayer in what few public schools existed in their day, our use of the history of their time must limit itself to broad purposes, not specific practices. By such a standard . . . the devotional exercises carried on in the Baltimore and Abington schools offend the First Amendment because they sufficiently threaten in our day those substantive evils the fear of which called forth the Establishment Clause of the First Amendment. . . . Our interpretation of the First Amendment must necessarily be responsive to the much more highly charged nature of religious questions in contemporary society.

Fourth, the American experiment in free public education available to all children has been guided in large measure by the dramatic evolution of the religious diversity among the population which our public schools serve. The interaction of these two important forces in our national life has placed in bold relief certain positive values in the consistent application to public institutions generally, and public schools particularly, of the constitutional decree against official involvements of religion which might produce the evils the Framers meant to forestall. The public schools are supported entirely, in most communities, by public funds—funds exacted not only from parents, nor alone from those who hold particular religious views, nor indeed from those who subscribe to any creed at all. It is implicit in the history and character of American public education that the schools serve a uniquely *public* function: the training of American citizens in an atmosphere free of parochial, divisive, or separatist influences of any sort—an atmosphere in which children may assimilate a heritage common to all American groups and religions. . . . This is a heritage neither theistic nor atheistic but simply civic and patriotic. . . .

Attendance at public schools never has been compulsory; parents remain morally and constitutionally free to choose the academic environment in which they wish their children to be educated. The relationship of the Establishment Clause . . . to the public school system is preeminently that of reserving such a choice to the individual parent, rather than vesting it in the majority of voters of each State or school district. The choice which is thus preserved is between a public secular education with its uniquely democratic values, and some form of private, or sectarian education, offering values of its own. In my judgment the First Amendment forbids the State to inhibit that freedom of choice by diminishing the attractiveness of either alternative—either by restricting the liberty of the private schools to inculcate whatever values they wish, or by jeopardizing the freedom of the public school from private or sectarian pressures. The choice between these very different forms of education is one—very much like the choice of whether to worship or not—which our Constitution leaves to the individual parent. It is no proper function of the state or local government to influence or restrict that election. The lesson of history—drawn more from the experiences of other countries than from our own—is that a system of free public education forfeits its unique contribution to the growth of democratic citizenship when that choice ceases to be freely available to each parent.

After an exhaustive and lengthy review of previous Supreme Court decisions interpreting the First Amendment, Justice Brennan examines the previous rulings of the Court making the provisions of the First Amendment applicable to the States under the provisions of the Fourteenth Amendment. The opinion then continues:

I turn now to the cases before us. The religious nature of the exercises here challenged seems plain. Unless *Engel* v. *Vitale* is to be overruled, or we are to engage in wholly disingenuous distinctions, we cannot sustain these practices. Daily recital of the Lord's Prayer and the reading of passages of Scripture are quite as clearly breaches of the command of the Establishment Clause as was the daily use of the rather bland Regents' Prayer in the New York public schools. Indeed, I would suppose that if anything the Lord's Prayer and the Holy Bible are more clearly sectarian, and the present violations of the First Amendment consequently more serious. But the religious exercises challenged in these cases have a long history. And almost from the beginning, Bible reading and daily prayer in the schools have been the subject of debate, criticism by educators and other public officials, and proscription by courts and legislative councils. At the outset, then, we must carefully canvass both aspects of this history. The use of prayers and Bible readings at the opening of the school day long antedates the founding of our Republic. The rules of the New Haven Hopkins Grammar School required in 1684 "that the Scholars being called together, the Mr. shall every morning begin his work with a short prayer for a blessing on his Laboures and their learning. . . ." More rigorous was the provision in a 1682 contract with a Dutch schoolmaster in Flatbush, New York: "When the school begins, one of the children shall read the morning prayer, as it stands in the catechism, and close with the prayer before dinner; in the afternoon it shall begin with the prayer after dinner, and end with the evening prayer. The evening school shall begin with the Lord's Prayer and close by singing a psalm."

After the Revolution, the new States uniformly continued these long established practices in the private and the few public grammar schools. The school committee of Boston in 1789, for example, required the city's several schoolmasters "daily to commence the duties of their office by prayer and reading a portion of the Sacred Scriptures. . . ." That requirement was mirrored throughout the original States and exemplified the universal practice well into the nineteenth century. As the free public schools gradually supplanted the private academies and sectarian schools between 1800 and 1850, morning devotional exercises were retained with few alterations. Indeed, public pressures upon school administrators in many parts of the country would hardly have condoned abandonment of practices to which a century or more of private religious education had accustomed the American people.

The controversy centered, in fact, principally about the elimination of plainly sectarian practices and textbooks, and led to the eventual substitution of nonsectarian, though still religious, exercises and materials.

Statutory provision for daily religious exercises is, however, of quite recent origin. At the turn of this century, there was but one State—Massachusetts—which had a law making morning prayer or Bible reading obligatory. Statutes elsewhere permitted such practices or simply left the question to local option. It was not until after 1910 that 11 more States, within a few years, joined Massachusetts in making one or both exercises compulsory. The Pennsylvania law with which we are concerned in the *Schempp* case, for example, took effect in 1913; and even the Rule of the Baltimore School Board involved in the *Murray* case dates only from 1905. In no State has there ever been a constitutional or statutory prohibition against the recital of prayers or the reading of Scripture, although a number of States have outlawed these practices by judicial decision or administrative order. What is noteworthy about the panoply of state and local regulations from which these cases emerge is the relative recency of the statutory codification of practices which have ancient roots and the rather small number of States which have ever prescribed compulsory religious exercises in the public schools.

The purposes underlying the adoption and perpetuation of these practices are somewhat complex. It is beyond question that the religious benefits and values realized from daily prayer and Bible reading have usually been considered paramount, and sufficient to justify the continuation of such practices. To Horace Mann, embroiled in an intense controversy over the role of sectarian instruction and textbooks in the Boston public schools, there was little question that regular use of the Bible—which he thought essentially nonsectarian—would bear fruit in the spiritual enlightenment of his pupils. A contemporary of Mann's, the Commissioner of Education of a neighboring State, expressed a view which many enlightened educators of that day shared:

"As a textbook of morals the Bible is pre-eminent and should have a prominent place in our schools either as a reading book or as a source of appeal and instruction. Sectarianism, indeed, should

not be countenanced in the schools; but the Bible is not sectarian
. . . The Scriptures should at least be read at the opening of school,
if no more. Prayer may also be offered with the happiest effects."

Wisconsin's Superintendent of Public Instruction, writing a few
years later, in 1858, reflected the attitude of his eastern colleagues,
in that he regarded "with special favor the use of the Bible in public
schools, as pre-eminently first in importance among text-books for
teaching the noblest principles of virtue, morality, patriotism, and
good order—love and reverence for God—charity and good will to
man."

Such statements reveal the understanding of educators that the
daily religious exercises in schools served broader goals than compelling formal worship of God or fostering church attendance. The
religious aims of the educators who adopted and retained such
exercises were comprehensive, and in many cases quite devoid of
sectarian bias—but the crucial fact is that they were nonetheless
religious. While it has been suggested, . . . that daily prayer and
reading of Scripture serve secular goals as well, there can be no
doubt that the origins of these practices were unambiguously religious, even where the educator's aim was not to win adherents to
a particular creed or faith.

The opinion next examines the history of controversy
in America over religious exercises in public schools and reaches
the conclusion that the doctrine expounded in *Engel* v. *Vitale*
was not really a novel one.

Almost from the beginning religious exercises in the public
schools have been the subject of intense criticism, vigorous debate,
and judicial or administrative prohibition. Significantly, educators
and school boards early entertained doubts about both the legality
and the soundness of opening the school day with compulsory
prayer or Bible reading. Particularly in the large Eastern cities,
where immigration had exposed the public schools to religious
diversities and conflicts unknown to the homogeneous academies
of the eighteenth century, local authorities found it necessary even
before the Civil War to seek an accommodation. In 1843, the
Philadelphia School Board adopted the following resolutions:

RESOLVED, that no children be required to attend or unite in the reading of the Bible in the Public Schools, whose parents are conscientiously opposed thereto;

RESOLVED, that those children whose parents conscientiously prefer and desire any particular version of the Bible, without note or comment, be furnished with same.

A decade later, the Superintendent of Schools of New York State issued an even bolder decree that prayers could no longer be required as part of public school activities, and that where the King James Bible was read, Catholic students could not be compelled to attend. This type of accommodation was not restricted to the east Coast; the Cincinnati Board of Education resolved in 1869 that "religious instruction and the reading of religious books, including the Holy Bible are prohibited in the common schools of Cincinnati, it being the true object and intent of this rule to allow the children of parents of all sects and opinions, in matters of faith and worship to enjoy alike the benefit of the common school fund. . . ." The Board repealed at the same time an earlier regulation which had required the singing of hymns and psalms to accompany the Bible reading at the start of the school day. And in 1889, one commentator ventured the view that "there is not enough to be gained from Bible reading to justify the quarrel that has been raised over it."

Thus a great deal of controversy over religion in the public schools had preceded the debate over the Blaine Amendment, precipitated by President Grant's insistence that matters of religion should be left "to the family altar, the church, and the private school, supported entirely by private contributions." There was ample precedent, too, for Theodore Roosevelt's declaration that in the interest of "absolutely non-sectarian public schools" it was "not our business to have the Protestant Bible or the Catholic Vulgate or the Talmud read in those schools." The same principle appeared in a message of an Ohio Governor who vetoed a compulsory Bible-reading bill in 1925:

"It is my belief that religious teaching in our homes, Sunday schools, churches, by the good mothers, fathers and ministers of Ohio is far preferable to compulsory teaching of religion by the State. The spirit of our federal and state constitutions from the beginning . . . has left religious instruction to the discretion of the parents."

The same theme has recurred in the opinions of the Attorney Generals of several States holding religious exercises or instruction to be in violation of the state or federal constitutional command of separation of church and state. Thus the basic principle upon which our decision last year in *Engel* v. *Vitale* necessarily rested, and which we reaffirm today, can hardly be thought to be radical or novel. Particularly relevant for our purposes are the decisions of the state courts on questions of religion in the public schools. Those decisions, while not, of course, authoritative in this Court, serve nevertheless to define the problem before us and to guide our inquiry. With the growth of religious diversity and the rise of vigorous dissent it was inevitable that the courts would be called upon to enjoin religious practices in the public schools which offended certain sects and groups. The earliest of such decisions declined to review the propriety of actions by school authorities, so long as those actions were within the purview of the administrators' powers. Thus, where the local school board *required* religious exercises, the courts would not enjoin them; and where, as in at least one case, the school officials forbade devotional practices, the court refused on similar grounds to overrule that decision. Thus, whichever way the early cases came up the governing principle of nearly complete deference to administrative discretion effectively foreclosed any consideration of constitutional questions.

The last quarter of the nineteenth century found the courts beginning to question the constitutionality of public school religious exercises. The legal context was still, of course, that of the state constitutions, since the First Amendment had not yet been held applicable to state action. And the State constitutional prohibitions against church-state cooperation or governmental aid to religion were generally less rigorous than the Establishment Clause of the First Amendment. It is therefore remarkable that the courts of half a dozen States found compulsory religious exercises in the public schools in violation of their respective state constitutions. These courts attributed much significance to the clearly religious origins and content of the challenged practices, and to the impossibility of avoiding sectarian controversy in their conduct. . . . Even those state courts which have sustained devotional exercises under state law have usually recognized the primarily religious character of prayers and Bible readings. If such practices were not for that reason unconstitutional, it was necessarily because the state constitution forbade only public expenditures for *sectarian* instruction, or for activities which made the schoolhouse a "place of worship," but said nothing about the subtler question of laws "respecting an establishment of religion." Thus the panorama of history permits no other conclusion than that daily prayers and Bible reading in the public schools have always been designed to be, and have been regarded as, essentially religious exercises. . . .

Justice Brennan now discusses three contentions that had been advanced in support of the validity of the procedures under attack.

First, it is argued that however clearly religious may have been the origins and early nature of daily prayer and Bible reading, these practices today serve so clearly secular educational purposes that their religious attributes may be overlooked.

After a discussion of this contention, it is rejected by concluding:

. . . To the extent that only religious materials will serve this purpose, it seems to me that the purpose as well as the means is so plainly religious that the exercise is necessarily forbidden by the Establishment Clause. The fact that purely secular benefits may eventually result does not seem to me to justify the exercises, for similar indirect nonreligious benefits could no doubt have been claimed for the released time program invalidated in *McCollum.*

The second facet of this contention is described:

The second justification assumes that religious exercises at the start of the school day may directly serve solely secular ends—for example, by fostering harmony and tolerance among pupils, enhancing the authority of the teacher, and inspiring better discipline.

This contention after being discussed is also rejected:

While I do not question the judgment of experienced educators that the challenged practices may well achieve valuable secular ends, it seems to me that the State acts unconstitutionally if it either sets about to attain even indirectly religious ends by religious means, or if it uses religious means to serve secular ends where secular means would suffice.

The second contention is stated:

Second, it is argued that the particular practices involved in the two cases before us are unobjectionable because they prefer no particular sect or sects at the expense of others.

Justice Brennan analyzes and rejects this argument in the following language:

One answer, which might be dispositive, is that any version of the Bible is inherently sectarian, else there would be no need to offer a system of rotation or alternation of versions in the first place, that is, to allow different sectarian versions to be used on different days. The sectarian character of the Holy Bible has been at the core of the whole controversy over religious practices in the public schools throughout its long and often bitter history. To vary the version as the Abington and Baltimore schools have done may well be less offensive than to read from the King James version every day, as once was the practice. But the result even of this relatively benign procedure is that majority sects are preferred in approximate proportion to their representation in the community and in the student body, while the smaller sects suffer commensurate discrimination. So long as the subject matter of the exercise is sectarian in character, these consequences cannot be avoided.

The argument contains, however, a more basic flaw. There are persons in every community—often deeply devout—to whom any version of the Judaeo-Christian Bible is offensive. There are others whose reverence for the Holy Scriptures demands private study or reflection and to whom public reading or recitation is sacrilegious. . . . To such persons it is not the fact of using the Bible in the public schools, nor the content of any particular version, that is offensive, but only the manner in which it is used. For such persons, the anathema of public communion is even more pronounced when prayer is involved. Many deeply devout persons have always regarded prayer as a necessarily private experience. One Protestant group recently commented, for example: "When one thinks of prayer as a sincere outreach of a human soul to the Creator, 're-quired prayer' becomes an absurdity." There is a similar problem with respect to comment upon the passages of Scripture which are to be read. Most present statutes forbid comment, and this practice accords with the views of many religious groups as to the manner in which the Bible should be read. However, as a recent survey dis-closes, scriptural passages read without comment frequently convey no message to the younger children in the school. Thus there has developed a practice in some schools of bridging the gap between faith and understanding by means of "definitions" even where "comment" is forbidden by statute. The present practice therefore poses a difficult dilemma: While Bible reading is almost universally required to be without comment, since only by such prohibition can sectarian interpretation be excluded from the classroom, the rule breaks down at the point at which rudimentary definitions of Biblical terms are necessary for comprehension if the exercise is to be meaningful at all.

It has been suggested that a tentative solution to these problems may lie in the fashioning of a "common core" of theology tolerable to all creeds but preferential to none. But as one commentator has recently observed "history is not encouraging" to those who hope to fashion a "common denominator of religion detached from its manifestation in any organized church." . . . Thus the notion of a "common core" litany or supplication offends many deeply de-vout worshippers who do not find clearly sectarian practices objec-tionable. Father Gustave Weigel has recently stated a widely shared view: "The moral code held by each separate religious community can reductively be unified, but the consistent particular believer wants no such reduction." And, as the American Council on Edu-cation warned several years ago: "The notion of a common core suggests a watering down of the several faiths to the point where common essentials appear. This might easily lead to a new sect—a public school sect—which would take its place alongside the exist-ing faiths and compete with them." *Engel* is surely authority that nonsectarian religious practices, equally with sectarian exercises, violate the Establishment Clause. Moreover, even if the Establishment Clause were oblivious to nonsectarian religious practices, I think it quite likely that the "common core" approach would be sufficiently objectionable to many groups to be foreclosed by the prohibitions of the Free Exercise Clause.

The opinion also gives reasons for rejecting the third contention which rested on the excusal clause in the laws governing both cases.

Justice Brennan says in summary:

To summarize my views concerning the merits of these two cases: The history, the purpose, and the operation of the daily prayer recital and Bible reading leave no doubt that these practices standing by themselves constitute an impermissible breach of the Establishment Clause. Such devotional exercises may well serve legitimate nonreligious purposes. To the extent, however that such purposes are really without religious significance, it has never been demonstrated that secular means would not suffice. Indeed I would suggest that patriotic or other nonreligious materials might prove adequate substitutes—inadequate only to the extent that the purposes now served are indeed directly or indirectly religious. Under such circumstances, the States may not employ religious means to reach a secular goal unless secular means are wholly unavailing. . . .

The remaining ten pages of the opinion discuss the various other religious activities in government which it is argued would have to be abolished under this decision but which Justice Brennan says would not be affected. Since most of them do not directly affect school procedures they are not digested here except to quote that portion of the opinion dealing with the nondevotional use of the Bible in the public schools, concerning which it is said:

The holding of the Court today plainly does not foreclose teaching about the Holy Scriptures or about the differences between religious sects in literature or history classes. Whether or not the Bible is involved, it would be impossible to teach meaningfully many subjects in the social sciences or the humanities without some mention of religion. To what extent and to what points in the curriculum religious materials should be cited, are matters which the courts ought to entrust very largely to the experienced officials who superintend our Nation's public schools. They are experts in such matters and we are not. . . . We do not, however, in my view usurp the jurisdiction of school administrators by holding as we do today that morning devotional exercises in any form are constitutionally invalid. But there is no occasion now to go further and anticipate problems we cannot judge with the material now before us. Any attempt to impose rigid limits upon the mention of God or references to the Bible in the classroom would be fraught with dangers. If it should sometime hereafter be shown that in fact religion can play no part in the teaching of a given subject without resurrecting the ghost of the practices we strike down today, it will then be time enough to consider questions we must now defer.

JUSTICE GOLDBERG'S CONCURRING OPINION

In his concurring opinion, in which Justice Harlan joined, Justice Goldberg expressed his approval of the Court's decision:

The considerations which lead the Court today to interdict the clearly religious practices presented in these cases are to me wholly compelling; I have no doubt as to the propriety of the decision . . .

This opinion further states:

The First Amendment's guarantees, as applied to the States through the Fourteenth Amendment, foreclose not only laws "respecting an establishment of religion" but also those "prohibiting the free exercise thereof." These two proscriptions are to be read together, and in light of the single end which they are designed to serve. The basic purpose of the First Amendment is to promote and assure the fullest possible scope of religious liberty and tolerance for all and to nurture the conditions which secure the best hope of attainment of that end.

The fullest realization of true religious liberty requires that government neither engage in nor compel religious practices, that it effect no favoritism among sects or between religion and nonreligion, and that it work deterrence of no religious belief. But devotion even to these simply stated objectives presents no easy course, for the unavoidable accommodations necessary to achieve the maximum enjoyment of each and all of them are often difficult of discernment. There is for me no simple and clear measure which by precise application can readily and invariably demark the permissible from the impermissible.

It is said, and I agree, that the attitude of the state toward religion must be one of neutrality. But untutored devotion to the concept of neutrality can lead to invocation or approval of results which partake not simply of that non-interference and noninvolvement with the religious which the Constitution commands, but of a brooding and pervasive devotion to the secular and a passive, or even active, hostility to the religious. Such results are not only not compelled by the Constitution, but, it seems to me, are prohibited by it.

Neither the State nor this Court can or should ignore the significance of the fact that a vast portion of our people believe in and worship God and that many of our legal, political and personal values derive historically from religious teachings. Government must inevitably take cognizance of the existence of religion, and indeed, under certain circumstances the First Amendment may require that it do so. And it seems clear to me from the opinions of the present and past cases that the Court would recognize the propriety of providing military chaplains and of teaching about religion, as distinguished from the teaching of religion, in the public schools. The examples could readily be multiplied, for both the required and the permissible accommodations between state and church frame the relation as one free from hostility or favor and productive of religious and political harmony, but without undue involvement of one in the concerns or practices of the other. To be sure, the judgment in each case is a delicate one, but it must be made if we are to do loyal service as judges to the ultimate First Amendment objective of religious liberty. The practices here involved do not fall within any sensible or acceptable concept of compelled or permitted accommodation and involve the state so significantly and directly in the realm of the sectarian as to give rise to those very divisive influences and inhibitions of freedom which both religion clauses of the First Amendment preclude. The state has ordained and has utilized its facilities to engage in unmistakably religious exercises—the devotional reading and recitation of the Holy Bible—in a manner having substantial and significant import and impact. That it has selected, rather than written, a particular devotional liturgy seems to me without constitutional import. The pervasive religiosity and direct governmental involvement inhering in the prescription of prayer and Bible reading in the public schools, during and as part of the curricular day, involving young impressionable children whose school attendance is statutorily compelled and utilizing the prestige, power, and influence of school administration, staff and authority, cannot realistically be termed simply accommodation, and must fall within the interdiction of the First Amendment. I find nothing in the opinion of the Court which says more than this. And, of course, today's decision does not mean that all incidents of government which import of the religious are therefore and without more banned by the strictures of the Establishment Clause.

After quoting from the Court's opinion in *Engel* v. *Vitale,* Justice Goldberg concludes his opinion:

The First Amendment does not prohibit practices which by any realistic measure create none of the dangers which it is designed to prevent and which do not so directly or substantially involve the state in religious exercises or in the favoring of religion as to have meaningful and practical impact. It is of course true that great consequences can grow from small beginnings, but the measure of constitutional adjudication is the ability and willingness to distinguish between real threat and mere shadow.

JUSTICE STEWART'S DISSENTING OPINION

As he did in *Engel* v. *Vitale,* Justice Stewart dissented and as in that case he expressed disagreement with the Court's interpretation of the Establishment Clause:

. . . But I cannot agree with what seems to me the insensitive definition of the Establishment Clause contained in the Court's opinion, nor with the different, but, I think equally mechanistic definitions contained in the separate opinions which have been filed.

After briefly reviewing a number of related previous cases, Justice Stewart says:

It has become accepted that the decision in *Pierce* v. *Society of Sisters* . . . upholding the right of parents to send their children to nonpublic schools, was ultimately based upon the recognition of the validity of the free exercise claim involved in that situation. It might be argued here that parents who wanted their children to be exposed to religious influences in school could, under *Pierce*, send their children to private or parochial schools. But the consideration which renders this contention too facile to be determinative has already been recognized by the Court: "Freedom of speech, freedom of the press, freedom of religion are available to all, not merely to those who can pay their own way." . . . It might also be argued that parents who want their children exposed to religious influences can adequately fulfill that wish off school property and outside school time. With all its surface persuasiveness, however, this argument seriously misconceives the basic constitutional justification for permitting the exercises at issue in these cases. For a compulsory state educational system so structures a child's life that if religious exercises are held to be an impermissible activity in schools, religion is placed at an artificial and state-created disadvantage. Viewed in this light, permission of such exercises for those who want them is necessary if the schools are to be truly neutral in the matter of religion. And a refusal to permit religious exercises thus is seen, not as the realization of state neutrality, but rather as the establishment of a religion of secularism, or at least, as government support of the beliefs of those who think that religious exercises should be conducted only in private. What seems to me to be of paramount importance, then, is recognition of the fact that the claim advanced here in favor of Bible reading is sufficiently substantial to make simple reference to the constitutional phrase "establishment of religion" as inadequate an analysis of the cases before us as the ritualistic invocation of the nonconstitutional phrase "separation of church and state." What these cases compel, rather, is an analysis of just what the "neutrality" is which is required by the interplay of the Establishment and Free Exercise Clauses of the First Amendment . . .

In support of his view that the two cases should have been remanded to the lower courts for the taking of further evidence, Justice Stewart's opinion continues:

The dangers both to government and to religion inherent in official support of instruction in the tenets of various religious sects are absent in the present cases, which involve only a reading from the Bible unaccompanied by comments which might otherwise constitute instruction. Indeed, since, from all that appears in either record, any teacher who does not wish to do so is free not to participate, it cannot even be contended that some infinitesimal part of the salaries paid by the State are made contingent upon the performance of a religious function.

In the absence of evidence that the legislature or school board intended to prohibit local schools from substituting a different set of reading where parents requested such a change, we should not assume that the provisions before us—as actually administered—may not be construed simply as authorizing religious exercises, nor that the designations may not be treated simply as indications of the promulgating body's view as to the community's preference. We are duty bound to interpret these provisions so as to render them constitutional if reasonably possible. . . . In the *Schempp* case there is evidence which indicates that variations were in fact permitted by the very school there involved, and that further variations were not introduced only because of the absence of requests from parents. And in the *Murray* case the Baltimore rule itself contains a provision permitting another version of the Bible to be substituted for the King James version.

If the provisions are not so construed, I think that their validity under the Establishment Clause would be extremely doubtful, because of the designation of a particular religious book and a denominational prayer. But since, even if the provisions are construed as I believe they must be, I think that the cases before us must be remanded for further evidence on other issues—thus affording the plaintiffs an opportunity to prove that local variations are not in fact permitted. I shall for the balance of this dissenting opinion treat the provisions before us as making the variety and content of the exercises, as well as a choice as to their implementation, matters which ultimately reflect the consensus of each local school community. In the absence of coercion upon those who do not wish to participate—because they hold less strong beliefs, other beliefs, or no beliefs at all—such provisions cannot, in my view, be held to represent the type of support of religion barred by the Establishment Clause. For the only support which such rules provide for religion is the withholding of state hostility—a simple acknowledgement on the part of secular authorities that the Constitution does not require extirpation of all expression of religious belief.

I have said that these provisions authorizing religious exercises are properly to be regarded as measures making possible the free exercise of religion. But it is important to stress that, strictly speaking, what is at issue here is a privilege rather than a right. In other words, the question presented is not whether exercises such as those at issue here are constitutionally compelled, but rather whether they are constitutionally invalid. And that issue, in my view, turns on the question of coercion.

It is clear that the dangers of coercion involved in the holding of religious exercises in a schoolroom differ qualitatively from those presented by the use of similar exercises or affirmations in ceremonies attended by adults. Even as to children, however, the duty laid upon government in connection with religious exercises in the public schools is that of refraining from so structuring the school environment as to put any kind of pressure on a child to participate in those exercises; it is not that of providing an atmosphere in which children are kept scrupulously insulated from any awareness that some of their fellows may want to open the school day with prayer, or of the fact that there exist in our pluralistic society differences of religious belief.

The governmental neutrality which the First and Fourteenth Amendments require in the cases before us, in other words, is the extension of even-handed treatment to all who believe, doubt, or disbelieve—a refusal on the part of the State to weight the scales of private choice. In these cases, therefore, what is involved is not state action based on impermissible categories, but rather an attempt by the State to accommodate those differences which the existence in our society of a variety of religious beliefs makes inevitable. The Constitution requires that such efforts be struck down only if they are proven to entail the use of the secular authority of government to coerce a preference among such beliefs. It may well be, as has been argued to us, that even the supposed benefits to be derived from noncoercive religious exercises in public schools are incommensurate with the administrative problems which they would create. The choice involved, however, is one for each local community and its school board, and not for this Court. For, as I have said, religious exercises are not constitutionally invalid if they simply reflect differences which exist in the society from which the school draws its pupils. They become constitutionally invalid only if their administration places the sanction of secular authority behind one or more religious or irreligious beliefs. To be specific, it seems to me clear that certain types of exercises would present situations in which no possibility of coercion on the part of secular officials could be claimed to exist. Thus, if such exercises were held either before or after the official school day, or if the school schedule were such that participation were merely one among a number of desirable alternatives, it could hardly be contended that the exercises did anything more than to provide an opportunity for the voluntary expression of religious belief. On the other hand, a law which provided for religious exercises during the school day and which contained no excusal provision would obviously be unconstitutionally coercive upon those who did not wish to participate. And even under a law containing an excusal provision, if the exercises were held during the school day, and no equally desirable alternative were provided by the school authorities, the likelihood that children might be under at least some psychological compulsion to participate would be great. In a case such as the latter, however, I think we would err if we assumed such coercion in the absence of any evidence.

Justice Stewart's dissenting opinion concludes:

Viewed in this light, it seems to me clear that the records in both cases before us are wholly inadequate to support an informed or responsible decision. Both cases involved provisions which explicitly permit any student who wishes, to be excused from participation in the exercises. There is no evidence in either case as to whether there would exist any coercion of any kind upon a student who did not want to participate . . . In the *Schempp* case the record shows no more than a subjective prophecy by a parent of what he thought would happen if a request were made to be excused from participation in the exercises under the amended statute. No such request was ever made, and there is no evidence whatever as to what might or would actually happen, nor of what administrative arrangements the school actually might or could make to free from pressure of any kind those who did not want to participate in the exercises. . . .

What our Constitution indispensably protects is the freedom of each of us, be he Jew or Agnostic, Christian or Atheist, Buddhist or Free thinker, to believe or disbelieve, to worship or not worship, to pray or keep silent, according to his own conscience, uncoerced and unrestrained by government. It is conceivable that these school boards, or even all school boards, might eventually find it impossible to administer a system of religious exercises during school hours in such a way as to meet this constitutional standard—in such a way as completely to free from any kind of official coercion those who do not affirmatively want to participate. But I think we must not assume that boards so lack the quality of inventiveness and good will as to make impossible the achievement of that goal.

THE FLORIDA SUPREME COURT RULES AGAIN ON *CHAMBERLIN*

In January of 1964 an opinion was delivered on behalf of a unanimous Florida Supreme Court. This case, it will be recalled, had been rather summarily dealt with by the Supreme Court of the United States in June, 1963, at which time it was remanded to the State Court.

The opinion opens with the statement:

We have read with care and considered the opinions cited. Being in doubt as to the manner and extent to which our judgment should by reason thereof be modified, we permitted the State, through the Attorney General, to file a brief *amicus curiae* and requested of counsel further briefing and argument incident to our disposition of the reversal.

The view is expressed that the facts of the *Chamberlin* case were dissimilar to those in the *Schempp* and *Murray* cases "although it is noted, the Supreme Court of the United States declined to permit the filing of briefs and denied the request of counsel to argue the cause."

The Court states that it can see no reason to change its former ruling regarding baccalaureate services, religious censuses of pupils, and religious qualifications for hiring of teachers, as none of these issues were involved in *Schempp*. In addition the Court makes the point that plaintiffs had no standing to sue in reference to these issues as they were not directly affected.

The Court then quotes the relevant Florida statute as follows:

Whereas, it is in the interest of good moral training, of a life of honorable thought and good citizenship, that the public school children should have lessons of morality brought to their attention during their school days, therefore be it enacted . . ."

The Court then gives its reasons for distinguishing this case from those decided in the Supreme Court of the United States as follows:

It is our conclusion that the statute was founded upon secular rather than sectarian considerations and is to be construed as was the Sunday closing law in the *McGovern* case 366 U.S. 420. The statute, designed to require moral training and the inculcation of good citizenship does not offend the establishment clause of the Constitution as written and intended by its authors. The accommodation of religious beliefs is secondary to the intent of the Legislators. Since the intent of the Florida Legislature is apparent and the intent of the Pennsylvania and Maryland Legislatures is not disclosed, we think that the Florida statute poses a different problem and is not summarily stricken by the *Murray* and *Schempp* decisions.

The Court in milder language than that used in its original decision nevertheless clearly expresses its distaste for the reasoning employed by the Supreme Court of the United States:

In view of the dissimilarities of the facts here and those of the *Schempp* and *Murray* cases and our conviction that the establishment clause of the Constitution was never designed to prohibit the practices complained of, we do not feel that the privilege or duty, is ours to speculate the extent to which the Supreme Court of the United States intended to expound its philosophy. We have, without avail, endeavored to find, in the diverse views expressed by the several justices of the United States Supreme Court who participated in these decisions, a clear course for us to follow. It seems, therefore, more fitting that the responsibility for any enlargement be left to that Court.

TO THE SUPREME COURT ONCE MORE

As a result of this the *Chamberlin* case was again left to the Supreme Court of the United States. On June 1, 1964, that Court ruled:

The judgment of the Florida Supreme Court is reversed with respect to the issues of the constitutionality of prayer and of devotional Bible reading pursuant to a Florida statute . . .

In support of this ruling the Court cited *Schempp*. As to the other questions raised, the appeal was dismissed "for want of properly presented federal questions."

Justice Douglas, with whom Justice Black concurred, felt that the plaintiffs as taxpayers had standing to question the validity of baccalaureate services, a religious census among pupils, and a religious test for teachers (applicants for teaching positions were required to answer the question: "Do you believe in God?"). Justice Douglas felt that a substantial question was presented in the last of these issues and favored its being considered by the Court.

Justice Stewart advocated consideration on the merits of the prayer and Bible reading as well.

SUMMARY

1. Three cases involving religious exercises in public school classrooms reached the Supreme Court of the United States during the October 1962 term.

2. *Schempp* v. *Abington* arose in Pennsylvania where a state statute required reading of verses from the Bible in public school classrooms. The United States District Court, where the case was originally tried, ruled that this statutory requirement was in violation of the Establishment Clause of the First Amendment. The case was appealed to the Supreme Court. While the case was on appeal, the Pennsylvania state legislature amended the statute to provide for the excusal of those who did not wish to participate. The Supreme Court remanded the case to the District Court to determine whether this amendment would alter that court's view of the conflict of the statute with the United States Constitution. This action was erroneously interpreted by some as an indication that the Supreme Court felt that the amended statute was constitutional. On retrial the statute was again held to violate the First Amendment and an appeal once more was taken to the Supreme Court.

3. *Murray* v. *Curlett* arose in Maryland and involved the constitutionality of a requirement that the Bible be read and a prayer be said in public school classrooms. The regulation contained an excusal clause. The Court of Appeals of Maryland decided by a 4-to-3 majority that there was no constitutional objection to such a regulation. The case was then carried to the Supreme Court of the United States.

4. *Chamberlin* v. *Dade County*, which arose in Florida, involved the constitutionality of a number of religious practices: reading of the Bible, comments on the Bible, distribution of

sectarian literature to pupils, Bible instruction in the school building after school hours, recitation of sectarian prayers, observance of religious holidays, displaying of religious symbols, holding of baccalaureate services, conducting a religious census of children; and using religious tests in appointing and promoting teaching personnel. Some of the practices complained of were held to be unconstitutional by the Florida trial court. An appeal was taken to the Florida Supreme Court which in an opinion marked by its caustic comments concerning decisions of the Supreme Court of the United States, upheld the constitutionality of the practices laid before it on appeal. The case was then carried to the Supreme Court of the United States.

5. The Supreme Court accepted jurisdiction of the *Schempp* and *Murray* cases and on June 17, 1963, handed down its decision.

6. Justice Clark delivered the opinion on behalf of the 8-to-1 majority and declared that the practices complained of were unconstitutional under the terms of the Establishment Clause of the First Amendment. Justice Clark traced the religious influences in American life and the importance attached to religious freedom in a pluralistic society. Neutrality on the part of government toward religion, the opinion states, is part of our heritage. The ruling was against religious exercises in the public schools, but not against the study of either comparative religion or the history of religion. Concurring opinions were rendered by Justices Douglas, Brennan, and Goldberg, while Justice Stewart dissented.

7. The *Chamberlin* case was summarily remanded to the Florida Supreme Court. After this Court had reaffirmed the validity of the practices complained of, the case once more reached the Supreme Court of the United States. In June, 1964, that Court reversed the ruling insofar as prayer and Bible reading were concerned but did not pass on the other issues raised.

CHAPTER 9

IN RETROSPECT

THE SUPREME COURT of the United States occupies a unique role in our society. No parallel to this role can be found in any other time or place. Nine men, appointed for life by the President with the consent of the Senate, have the responsibility for setting social policy in many areas without authority to do so except insofar as this social policy is determined by their legal interpretation of the laws and the Constitution of the United States in the light of present-day needs. Unless the Court itself reverses its ruling in a later case, an event which happens very rarely, there is, in the last analysis, only one appeal from a Supreme Court decision and that is to the process of amending the Constitution. This process is long, difficult, and infrequently successful. The word of the Supreme Court is, therefore, in most cases the final one. It must be accepted, graciously or ungraciously as the case may be, by all other components of American society.

It is not at all surprising that many of the major constitutional decisions of the Supreme Court are unpopular when one considers that it is almost invariably a minority that seeks the protection of its constitutional rights. It is worth noting that in each of the 12 cases excerpted it was a minority group that brought about the Court's decision. Because the protection of the minority so frequently involves the majority, there is often a pained outcry. While the Supreme Court proceeds with great caution and seeks to avoid meeting any issue except when it becomes necessary, it has always been the view of this body that no entering wedge shall be allowed in the matter of a clear violation of a constitutional right.

REVIEW OF THE CASES EXCERPTED

In *Meyer v. Nebraska* the issue presented was the validity of a state law prohibiting the teaching of foreign languages in the nonpublic elementary schools. Clearly, it was the majority sentiment in those states passing such laws that Americanization would be promoted by such laws. As has been previously noted, no direct religious question was raised, but actually the schools involved were almost all religiously supported and operated. The Supreme Court held these laws to be beyond the constitutional powers of a state and thus preserved the rights of private schools, whether religiously oriented or not, to determine the content of their curricula. This decision did not imply any impotence on the part of the state in the matter of requiring inclusion of material in that curriculum but dealt solely with exclusion.

In *Pierce v. Society of Sisters*, the law requiring all children to attend public school had been adopted by a clear majority of the voters of the State of Oregon. While it is true that this law did not single out religious schools, it was clear to all concerned that religiously oriented schools were the target. Here, as in the *Meyer* case, no mention was made either in the arguments or in the Court's decision of the First Amendment, but in later cases the point is made over and over again that because of this case there is no justification for religious instruction or exercises in the public school classroom.

The only cases decided by the Supreme Court that concern the question of "free exercise" and the schools are those involving compulsory saluting of the flag. Once more it was an expression of the majority will that brought about the adoption of laws and regulations requiring all public school pupils to participate in giving the Pledge of Allegiance to the Flag. The members of the Jehovah's Witnesses sect who found participation in this ceremony to be in conflict with their religious beliefs represented a very small sector of our population. A sharp difference is found between these cases and the *Engel* and *Schempp* cases. Here the Supreme Court held that excusing the objecting children from participation was all that was required, but in the subsequent cases involving devotional exercises the Court held that excusal did not serve to adequately protect the rights of the minority group. The reason for the different holdings clearly lies in the fact that the flag salute cases involved the Free Exercise Clause of the First Amendment while the prayer cases turned on an interpretation of the Establishment Clause.

Just as excusal was held insufficient protection of constitutional rights in the later prayer cases, so in *McCollum* excusal was held not to properly protect the rights of the small minority who did not wish to participate in sectarian religious instruction given in the public school classroom during school hours. The *Zorach* case also involved the appeal of a minority but in this case the ruling was in favor of the majority when the Court held dismissal from school for the purpose of attending sectarian religious instruction elsewhere during school hours to be constitutionally unobjectionable.

The *Cochran* case which did not turn on the First Amendment and the *Everson* case which the Court used as an occasion for its most thorough analysis of the Establishment Clause established the important principle of "child-benefit." It is, of course, obvious that any help, financial or otherwise, given to a parochial school child tends directly or indirectly to aid the parochial school itself as this then becomes a service that that school need not render. By the same token, when the government assumes an expense that would otherwise be a parental one, the parochial school is benefited at least indirectly by the resulting greater share of parental resources available to it. It is, however, exceedingly difficult to draw the line between a governmental expenditure on behalf of the child and one on behalf of the parochial school. Extremes are easily interpreted but in the middle group this becomes an exceedingly sticky question. A few more words will be said about the child-benefit theory later in this chapter.

The last four cases excerpted here deal with devotional exercises in the public school classroom. *Engel* v. *Vitale* stirred the most controversy but actually the decision in that case was the mildest and most restricted of the four. Considerable doubt existed for a year after the decision as to whether the Court would or would not extend the doctrine of that case. *Engel* turned largely on the fact that the prayer in question had been composed by a state agency and there was no intimation one way or another as to the Court's views on Bible reading or on prayers not composed by state agencies.

Schempp and *Murray* squarely presented the Court with the validity of Bible reading and praying in the public school classroom. The Court unequivocally held such activities violative of the Establishment Clause of the First Amendment. Surprisingly, the reaction to the decision in these cases was not nearly so furious and volatile as the reaction had been to *Engel*. This does not imply that it was a popular decision or that the groups reacting unfavorably to *Engel* had been won over.

The *Chamberlin* case presented many issues about which there had been and still are great uncertainties, but in the last analysis the final decision dealt only with prayers and Bible reading and thus did not extend or restrict the *Schempp* ruling in any way whatsoever. The principal point of interest in this case lies in the byplay between the Florida Supreme Court's anxiety to display its deep-seated disagreement with the Su-

preme Court of the United States' interpretation of the Establishment Clause and the Supreme Court's summary disposition
of the case on two separate occasions.

The 12 cases included in this book show the result of a
chain of reasoning in which, to a remarkable degree, each case
gives support to the decision in the following one. It must be
borne in mind, however, that the view contrary to the one
adopted by the Court was upheld by learned counsel and almost
invariably by one or more members of the Court itself. To say
that these decisions were foreordained as an indisputable matter
of logic or reasoning would be rash indeed.

It can be argued that the series of decisions tends to have
a unifying effect on society in that diversity of opinion is respected and protected. It can also be argued that these decisions
have had the effect of polarizing the viewpoints of the factions
of society holding varying points of view as to the proper relationship between religion and the public school. Time will have
to pass before a fair judgment can be made as to which of these
arguments has the most validity. We are now too close to the
events to gain the necessary perspective.

CRITERIA EMPLOYED BY
THE COURT

Everson, the released time cases, and the prayer cases all
rest on the Court's interpretation of the Establishment Clause
of the First Amendment which states: "Congress shall make no
law respecting an establishment of religion." A great portion of
the decisions in these cases deal with attempted analysis of the
intentions of the "Founding Fathers" when they inserted this
provision into our Bill of Rights. There certainly is no incon-
trovertible evidence available as to exactly what these intentions
were. It is clear that at the time of the drafting and the adoption
of the Bill of Rights there was considerable concern lest the

newly created federal government usurp greater powers than its constituents intended to bestow upon it. It is also evident that there was strong feeling against the formation by that federal government of a state church supported by taxes and imposed on an unwilling populace.

There had been a great deal written about the intended strength of the concept referred to as the "wall of separation" between church and state, if indeed at the time that concept was generally accepted—which seems very doubtful. From extensive reading in this area one can only conclude that most of our Founding Fathers, if not all of them, would have been amazed at the interpretation now placed on this phrase. This does not mean, however, that they would necessarily be out of sympathy with this construction in the light of present-day conditions. It seems highly likely that men of the strong practical views of Madison and Jefferson would enthusiastically agree that the language of the Constitution should be interpreted in the light of existing conditions and current societal needs. The point would seem to be that the strongest support for the decisions in question does not necessarily come from the intentions of the framers of the Bill of Rights even if those intentions could be ascertained with any degree of certainty.

Similarly, without questioning the desirability of the interpretation given the Due Process Clause of the Fourteenth Amendment, it seems futile to seek historical evidence that its framers meant to incorporate the First Amendment's guarantees of religious freedom in the clause.

It is perfectly clear from the ruling of the Court on the five cases dealing with the Establishment Clause that there is no question about the interpretation of its meaning. There is an unequivocal and consistent view in these opinions to the effect that this clause demands an absolute separation between church and state. It seems most unlikely that the Court will, in the foreseeable future at least, depart to any extent from this view. The question that remains open is only whether a given activity impinges on this separation. In this respect it is not at all impossible that, in time, varying shades of interpretation may arise.

SOME UNRESOLVED MATTERS

The financial crisis facing education, caused by the unparalleled increase in population as well as by the needs of a technological age for trained personnel, is generally recognized as being very real. One solution not unanimously but generally agreed upon would be federal financial aid. This is not the place for an extended discussion of the arguments for and against federal aid. But one may point out that the absolute necessity in our technological era for educated workers combined with the high rate of mobility of our American population makes education of prime quality a matter of national rather than merely a state concern. The sad fact is that those states providing the most inadequate educational facilities are spending a larger proportion of their financial resources for education than are those with more satisfactory educational facilities. Federal aid could resolve this problem.

For many years bills proposing such federal aid have been introduced in Congress and just as often have failed of passage. Their failure can readily be attributed to an impasse between two groups. One faction insists that any aid given to public schools should be appropriated in equal proportions to nonpublic school children. The legality for this proposal is claimed on the basis of the child-benefit theory. The other faction insists with equal vehemence that any aid to other than public schools would be a violation of the Establishment Clause and would sound the death knell to American public education. One's opinion on the relative merits of these viewpoints does not affect the fact that federal aid to education bills are unlikely to be passed by the Congress in the foreseeable future unless some accommodation is reached between these viewpoints.

SHARED TIME

A possible, but surely not a certain, solution to this dilemma is embodied in a proposal that public schools taking part in "shared-time" programs be given financial aid from federal sources.[1] Because of the importance of resolving the present impasse on the federal aid question and because of the relevance of the decisions in this book to an intelligent appraisal of the constitutionality of the plan, this matter may be discussed at this point.

Shared time or dual enrolment is a plan whereby pupils of nonpublic schools enroll for part or even most of their school day in public school classes. This plan has been in effect on a small scale in some states for at least 20 years. Recently it has become more widespread. Also quite recent is the dramatic increase in the writings that have appeared in religious, lay, and educational journals advocating, opposing, and analyzing this plan.

While there is nothing in the nature of the plan that would limit it to Catholic parochial school pupils, it has in fact been generally so limited. This is not so surprising when one considers the fact that Catholic parochial schools form the largest segment of American nonpublic schools, as has already been noted. This implemented shared-time scheme actually means that parochial school pupils attend classes in so-called "neutral" subjects in the public school and are instructed in religion and in subjects having ethical aspects in the parochial school.

There are no accurate statistics available on how widespread this practice is but it is in effect to some extent in at least 280 school systems in 35 States, according to a survey made by

[1] Since this was written Congress, on April 11, 1965, passed a bill providing federal aid to education, an important feature of which is the provision for financial aid to programs of shared services.

the Research Division of the National Education Association. The number of pupils involved in some districts is exceedingly small but in the Pittsburgh school system, for example, over 5000 pupils are involved.

The benefits of the plan as advanced by its proponents may be summarized as follows:

1. The integration of diverse religious groups in public school classes aids the democratization which is one of the major purposes of the public school.
2. More pupils gain better educational training as some of the facilities used such as laboratories, etc. cannot be supplied in the private schools and would otherwise stand idle for a portion of the day.
3. Catholic parents who share in the tax burden supporting the public school gain some direct benefits from their contributions, while the public school maintains its tradition that it is open to all comers.
4. The public school gains support from parents of the private school pupils participating in this plan.
5. The contact between faculties and administrations of the two types of schools tends to improve educational practice in both.
6. The financial burden of the parochial school is eased, as are the demands on its physical facilities. It is thus able to accommodate more pupils and thereby able to satisfy the felt need of those parents wishing to obtain a religious education for their children.

Those who oppose shared-time plans point to a number of disadvantages. They may be summarized as follows:

1. There are insuperable administrative difficulties inherent in shared-time plans. Among them are scheduling, discipline, observation of holidays, accreditation, grading, and the maintenance of the proper relationship between two school systems having diverse purposes.

2. Divisiveness is strengthened rather than diminished by this plan.

3. Public school facilities are already overtaxed and this additional burden can only result in lowering the quality of education.

4. The large-scale adoption of this plan would lead to a proliferation of private schools, religious and secular, which would sound the death knell of the public school system as we now know it.

5. There would be a tendency to force a modification of the public school curriculum to meet the demands of the parochial school authorities.

6. The plan is unconstitutional under the *Everson* doctrine and clearly violates the provisions of the Establishment Clause of the First Amendment.

The crux of the debate lies in the question of the constitutionality of the shared-time plan under the First Amendment. There will be no final answer until the Supreme Court rules on this matter. Thus far there has been no effort to obtain such a test. A number of opinions have been rendered by state Attorney Generals. While there has been some conflict, the overwhelming majority of these opinions has been in favor of the constitutionality of shared time.

Three strong arguments support its constitutional validity:

1. No public funds would flow directly or indirectly to the parochial school. Separation is maintained just as it was in *Everson*.

2. The administration and spending of all public funds involved is kept under the complete control of the state. No jurisdiction in this respect is surrendered to the private school. Children attend the public school classes, part-time it is true, on the same basis as all other children, receive the

same instruction, and have the same rights and responsibilities as do all other public school pupils.
3. No religious use is made of state funds.

Those arguing that shared time would be in violation of the Establishment Clause maintain that:

1. The release of financial pressure on the parochial school is indeed using tax money to support religious purposes. The benefit would accrue as much to the parochial school as to the children.
2. The child-benefit theory cannot logically be intended to include this plan.

Despite the differences that exist in opinions concerning the desirability and the constitutionality of shared time, it would be difficult to argue that this plan does not deserve serious consideration by all who are concerned about reaching a satisfactory accommodation between the social forces representing public and private education.

CHILD-BENEFIT THEORY

Another unresolved issue is to what degree the child-benefit theory established in *Cochran* and *Everson* is likely to be maintained in the future. Attention has already been drawn to Justice Douglas' doubts as to the validity of this doctrine expressed in his concurring opinion in *Schempp* when he said:

My problem today would be uncomplicated but for *Everson v. Board of Education* . . . which allowed taxpayers' money to be used to pay "the bus fares of parochial school pupils" . . . The *Everson* case seems in retrospect to be out of line with the First Amendment. Its result is appealing, as it allows aid to be given to needy children. Yet, by the same token, public funds could be used to satisfy other needs of children in parochial schools—lunches, books, and tuition being obvious examples.

It is worth noting that of the present personnel on the bench of the Supreme Court only Justices Black and Douglas were on the Court when *Everson* was decided. There are those who feel that if a similar question were brought before the presently constituted Court the result would not necessarily be the same.

This feeling is based in part on the fact that state courts have not looked with favor on the child-benefit theory when they have been called upon to consider it in the light of state constitutional provisions. It is true that state court decisions are not in any sense binding on the Supreme Court of the United States but they can illustrate a trend of thought and reasoning. The fact is that since *Cochran* the child-benefit theory has been rejected and the provision of textbooks to parochial school children held invalid under state constitutional provisions of New York, South Dakota, and Washington. Only in Mississippi was it sustained. Similarly, in the case of furnishing transportation to parochial school children the highest courts of Iowa, Washington, New Mexico, Missouri, Alaska, and Wisconsin have rejected the child-benefit theory. Connecticut was the only state in which the opposite conclusion was reached.

STANDING TO SUE

It is a well-established principle of law that one cannot bring a suit unless he is in fact adversely affected by the government action he complains of. The reason for such a rule seems apparent. In its absence the courts would be subjected to a flood of lawsuits that would never cease.

This principle has been construed to deny a federal taxpayer the right to challenge a federal expenditure. This rule was laid down in *Frothingham* v. *Mellon* in 1923 and has never been reversed. A rather cogent argument can be advanced against this rule. Nevertheless, this rule could well be invoked to deny a taxpayer the right, for example, to challenge a federal bill giving aid to parochial schools.

On the other hand, the principle is well established that a state or local taxpayer who has standing under state law to challenge a substantial expenditure may have his case considered by the Supreme Court of the United States. The *Cochran* and *Everson* cases were brought by the plaintiffs in their capacities as state taxpayers.

In the *Doremus* case the state courts of New Jersey held that the plaintiff as a taxpayer had standing to challenge Bible reading in the schools but the Supreme Court of the United States held that the plaintiff-taxpayer could show no direct "dollars and cents injury." As far as the taxpayer was concerned, an additional expense was involved in the reading of the Bible in the school as compared to the reading of anything else.

In *McCollum, Zorach, Vitale,* and *Schempp* the standing of the plaintiffs depended not upon a financial consideration but on the potential injury to children currently in school and thus directly on the injury claimed by the parents of these children. In *Schempp,* for example, the Court said that the children and their parents were "directly affected by the laws and practices against which their claims were directed. These interests surely suffice to give the parties standing to complain."

The Supreme Court will not grant standing to parties bringing action to vindicate the public interest when they cannot show a legal interest of their own. Because of this a number of issues raised in *Chamberlin* are unlikely to be considered by the Supreme Court. Only those issues raised by a party whose interest is in protecting his child from what he deems to be unacceptable religious influence has standing to object to that influence. Otherwise the objection must be based on a challenge of a substantial public expenditure and then only when this expenditure is a state or a local one.

NEXT STEPS

Many of the practices held to be objectionable under the terms of the First Amendment by the Supreme Court will nevertheless continue in the classrooms of many public schools for some time to come. A Supreme Court decision is not self-enforcing and when such a procedure is not challenged there is nothing to prevent its continuance. In religiously homogeneous communities such challenges probably will never be made. Since, under such circumstances, no one is offended, probably no great harm can result. If, however, no objection is made by a minority because of pressure from the majority the situation is indeed most unfortunate and renders void the protection offered such minorities by our Bill of Rights.

There is a considerable body of opposition to the doctrines set forth by the Supreme Court in *Engel* and *Schempp*. It has been proposed by some who hold this view that the Constitution should be amended in such a way as to nullify these rulings. These proponents are well within their rights in making such a proposal and their action is not without adequate precedent. As a result, numerous proposed constitutional amendments have been introduced in the Congress and in 1964 lengthy hearings on this subject were held by a Committee of the House of Representatives. So far, no action on this matter has been taken by either House of Congress. Even if this amendment is proposed by Congress it will have to be ratified by at least 37 state legislatures in order to be adopted. Only future events can determine the fate of such an amendment but if an amendment to the Constitution is adopted in the legally prescribed manner its validity and propriety cannot be challenged.

WHAT IS NEEDED

In the last analysis the problems arising in a society marked by religious diversity cannot be resolved by court decisions. Often these decisions will exacerbate rather than ease tensions. Differences are accentuated and agreements minimized in the controversy that such decisions as *McCollum, Everson,* and *Engel* arouse.

What is needed in our society as a whole, but especially in matters pertaining to our schools, is a spirit of understanding and consideration toward those who hold religious views different from or even contrary to our own. Such a spirit must go far beyond that of tolerance for diverse views. A spirit of accommodation is, of course, as necessary on the part of those holding minority views as it is on the part of those professing generally accepted beliefs and views. Recriminations and reproaches will not solve any portion of our problem but frank discussions may. Above all else a free flow of information is essential. This free flow will prevent one cause of much irritation—disputes about matters that don't exist. If the presentation of the foregoing material contributes in any degree to such a free flow of information, it will have served its intended purpose.

TABLE OF CASES

SELECTED BIBLIOGRAPHY

American Association of School Administrators, *Religion in the Public Schools*, Washington, D.C.: American Association of School Administrators, 1964.

Blanshard, Paul, *Religion and the Schools*, Boston: Beacon Press, 1963.

Boles, Donald E., *The Bible, Religion, and the Public Schools*, Ames, Iowa: Iowa State University Press, 1961.

Brennan, William J., Jr., *The Bill of Rights and the States*, Santa Barbara, Calif.: Center for the Study of Democratic Institutions, 1961.

Brickman, William W. and Lehrer, Stanley (eds.), *Religion, Government and Education*, New York: Society for the Advancement of Education, 1961.

Fraenkel, Osmond K., *The Supreme Court and Civil Liberties*, Dobbs Ferry, N.Y.: Oceana Publications, 1963.

Kurland, Philip B., *Religion and the Law*, Chicago: Aldine Publishing Co., 1962.

McCluskey, Neil G., *Catholic Viewpoint on Education*, Garden City, N.Y.: Hanover House, 1959.

McGrath, John J. (ed.), *Church and State in American Law*, Milwaukee: Bruce Publishing Company, 1962.

Rutland, Robert Allen, *The Birth of the Bill of Rights 1776–1791*, Chapel Hill, N.C.: University of North Carolina Press, 1955.

INDEX

Boldface numbers indicate pages on which Supreme Court decisions appear.